CONSULTATIVE CLOSING

CONSULTATIVE CLOSING

Simple Steps That Build Relationships and Win Even the Toughest Sale

Greg Bennett

American Management Association

New York • Atlanta • Brussels • Chicago • Mexico City • San Francisco
Shanghai • Tokyo • Toronto • Washington, D.C.

Special discounts on bulk quantities of AMACOM books are available to corporations, professional associations, and other organizations. For details, contact Special Sales Department, AMACOM, a division of American Management Association, 1601 Broadway, New York, NY 10019.
Tel: 212-903-8316. Fax: 212-903-8083.
E-mail: specialsls@amanet.org
Website: www. amacombooks.org/go/specialsales
To view all AMACOM titles go to: www.amacombooks.org

This publication is designed to provide accurate and authoritative information in regard to the subject matter covered. It is sold with the understanding that the publisher is not engaged in rendering legal, accounting, or other professional service. If legal advice or other expert assistance is required, the services of a competent professional person should be sought.

Library of Congress Cataloging-in-Publication Data

Bennett, Greg
       Consultative closing : simple steps that build relationships and win even the toughest sale / Greg Bennett.
          p.   cm.
       Includes bibliographical references and index.
       ISBN-10: 0-8144-7399-7
       ISBN-13: 978-0-8144-7399-3
       1. Selling.   I. Title.

   HF5438.25.B448   2007
   658.85–dc22

                                                                2006012011

This book is dedicated to everyone who
has ever had to wake up
knowing they must sell an idea,
a product, a story, or a dream.
Your passion and courage
changed the world.

Contents

Acknowledgments

I should say "thank you" to every person I've ever known and worked with, because you've taught me in every way possible the lessons I needed to know to get to this place and to write this book (the first of what I hope will be many over the next several years). Without the experiences (both good and bad), without the knowledge, without the trust and faith—venturing down this path would not have been possible.

I also want to thank Dave Gardy of TVWorldwide and my agent William Brown. Special thanks to my editor at AMACOM, Christina Parisi, whose positive guidance and clear direction helped me focus on the critical points and not get lost in places I shouldn't wander.

Finally, a huge amount of gratitude to my wife Rosemary, who always believed in me and made tough choices with her career so that I could do what I do and to raise our girls the way we felt was important. And to my girls— Brooke, Blaire, Kaity, and Maddy—you are my inspiration for always reaching higher. To all my family and friends, especially my mother and father who gave me the gifts of creativity and humor; to my business partner Bob; to the associates at APC and KSE; and to the many wonderful clients I've worked with over the years: all of whom have encouraged me, supported me, and pushed me to share what I know with the world, *Thank you!*

CONSULTATIVE CLOSING

Introduction

I can make anyone a good closer. And I can make good closers *great* closers. Even if you're not particularly aggressive or quick on your feet or mesmerizing in front of a crowd, whether you've been in sales for twenty years or are brand new—I can improve your closing success without having to change your personality, or making you do things that you're not comfortable with or that put undo stress and pressure on your client. And if you're one of the many people who need to generate new business, but you don't like to call it "sales"—such as consultants, doctors, lawyers, or business owners—I can even make you a more effective closer, without turning you into a . . . "salesperson!" (*Ewwwww.* Nasty word, right?)

And I can show you how to become a better closer and build stronger client relationships at the same time. This is something most people struggle with because improving closing traditionally has meant increasing pressure, and increasing pressure usually leads to damaging relationships, not building and supporting them. But you can improve closing *and* improve relationships, and I am going to show

1

you some unique and very easy-to-implement steps you can put into place and start seeing results right away.

I make these dramatic claims not to be boastful, or to point out how wonderful I may think I am. This book is not about me, it's about you. My success only comes through your success. And it's through the evidence of my clients' successes that I am able to make the claims I do. I've done it every day of my professional career as a trainer and coach since 1988.

Another reason I'm so confident I can make anyone a better closer is that I've discovered a huge gap in how 99 percent of all salespeople and sales organizations go about the closing process. A huge gap. And once I gave them some simple steps for filling that gap, they immediately showed signs of improvement. Here's an early hint at the gap: *The gap is in the process–or lack of process really–for closing.*

We've made the mistake of thinking that closing is all about the people involved–the salesperson and the client–and what they're saying to each other as they go through this "dance." And, of course, the people and what they're saying are important areas, and we'll discuss ways to improve what we say and how we listen to people. But these things aren't as important as having an effective process or plan in place for taking a client through the closing stages–before, during, and after the sale. The lack of a definite closing process in place is stalling sales careers and literally killing sales organizations.

NO ONE REALLY FOCUSES ON THE CLOSING PROCESS: NOT EVEN PEOPLE WHO CALL THEMSELVES "CONSULTATIVE SALESPEOPLE"

As a trainer, consultant, and coach, I've worked with hundreds of sales organization and thousands of salespeople.

I've worked with experienced, high-income sales people, and I've worked with right-out-of-school rookies. I've worked with innovative, dynamic sales managers, and I've worked with boring dinosaurs, angrily stomping around and waiting to just lie down and die. I can honestly say in all my years of working in and around these folks, I never once came upon an individual, a manager, or a company that had the closing process really defined and in place—not one!

Even people who went to great lengths to tell me they were more of a "consultant" than a "salesperson," and that they practiced "consultative selling" (which I agree is the only way to sell, and we'll get into all that later on in this book), even these folks were missing the boat when it came to having an effective closing process.

Everyone thinks they have a sales process: "We call on clients; do a needs analysis; discover areas of need, pain, objectives; come up with customized solutions; then try to get them to take action. That's our process." What they're really doing is actively engaging in selling—and actively trying to close—but it's not a defined closing process. They're missing something, and they don't even realize it.

This is why I can say with confidence that I can make anyone a better closer. And that's why I know you'll become a better closer too by following the secrets I've outlined in this book. I am absolutely certain of it.

LACK OF PROCESS IS ONLY PART OF THE PROBLEM WITH CLOSING FOR CONSULTATIVE SALESPEOPLE

Beyond lack of process, there are several other reasons why Carl "the Consultative Seller" can't close, and we will attempt to address a few of the more prominent ones in this book. Some have to do with the way people act when they're playing the role of client in a sales call. Others have to do with how salespeople have a tendency to avoid reality and choose instead to live in a pretend world, with opportunities that don't really exist.

A major area of focus will be on the abysmal performance of salespeople after the sale is completed. Just as clients are getting excited and wanting to form long-term relationships with sellers, the sellers are running the other way, moving on to the next opportunity. The simple steps we'll focus on in this area will go a long way to forming much better client relationships.

So even though the development of a closing process is the most important concept we're going to review in this book, we're also going to work together on these other core problem areas that keep many consultative salespeople from becoming great *consultative closers.*

And we really do need to be focused on closing, because the pressure to close—and close quickly—has never been greater. Have you noticed a heightened sense of urgency in your world? It seems we're always under the gun to do more, and do it faster?

Where this sudden increase in pressure to close is coming from I'm not exactly sure—I've had clients tell me everything from an increase in global competition, to new acquisitions putting the pressure on income, to antsy stockholders who live or die based on quarterly returns. Whatever the reason, we all need to be focused on becoming more efficient and effective in the closing process. And we better learn it now. Today!

But we need to be careful about how we go about turning up the closing pressure. As consultative sales professionals, we've gone to great lengths to emphasize our desire to form lasting relationships with clients. I hope we've done an effective job of understanding their needs, and that we have developed customized solution options that address those needs. We need to learn how to apply the right amount of pressure without acting in a "counter culture" way. We need to learn how to close without ruining the relationship. We need to get people to take action, without making them doubt our motives. And we need a way to do it all without having to become something we personally can't stand.

A gentleman in one of my recent seminars said it best: "I struggle with just hitting the switch and going from being a client's best buddy, with whom I've worked to form a good relationship, to suddenly turning into Mr. Hammer Closer—just because corporate has said we need to get sales in the door NOW."

We need to find a way to bridge the gap between consultant and closer, and we need to do it quickly.

The good news is, I can make anyone a better closer! And we can do it quickly together. Let's get started.

WHAT YOU ARE GOING TO WALK AWAY WITH

- You'll see plainly how "consultative selling," though it is the way we must be selling now and in the future, may have inadvertently led to problems in the closing stages of the sales process.

- You'll see "closing" in an entirely new light, and you will see how your old paradigm may have put blinders on what truly is going on in the process.

- You'll discover that the closing process all boils down to VERBAL versus ACTION, and how our inclination to live in a "verbal-only" world is causing the bulk of the sales problems not only for salespeople, but for sales managers, top management, and ownership.

- You'll learn all about "The Process," or what I call the "Mini-Steps": that "secret" strategy no one is doing, as I mentioned earlier. This segment will have you shaking your head, saying, "This makes so much sense, why didn't I see this before?"

- You'll be able to come up with your own Closing Process and learn how to develop effective Closing Plans.

- You'll learn about the horrible world of MAYBE, where clients and salespeople love to coexist in a sick and dysfunctional dance that ends up causing some very hurt feelings and destroyed careers. I call it the "Death Valley of Indecision."

- You'll learn to love NO as the number one tool for closing on opportunities and either advancing the sale, or moving out the "dead weight."

- You'll learn how to close on long-term relationships with clients by developing a "maximization program."

- You'll learn how to use Mini-Steps after the sale to lock the client down and keep the competition away.

- You'll learn some of my core concepts on prospecting and time maximization, and how we can waste a tremendous amount of time on prospects that will NEVER close.

- You'll learn some strategies for building and supporting an effective network of professionals. These people will help you fish for opportunities that are much closer to "closed" before they ever hit the net.

SOME BOTTOM-LINE BENEFITS YOU WILL SEE

- You will be able to close more effectively without changing your personality or becoming something you're not (pushy, mean, etc.).

- You will be able to close more quickly.

- You will be a better judge of what is in your sales pipeline and stop the guessing game that can bog you down and may hurt your career.

- You will form deeper bonds with clients *as* you're closing: Before, During, and After the closing process.

- You will have more fun, make more money, and be able to dream even greater dreams.

HOW BEST TO ATTACK THIS BOOK

I think learning new sales concepts and strategies, whether from a book or in a sales seminar, can be like eating cotton candy: The new ideas are fun, different, and of good consistency; they can give you a great temporary buzz, but it all disappears pretty quickly once ingested. We've all seen the surveys that show that 80 or 90 percent of what you learn in a workshop is gone by the next day!! (FYI: This is why trainers get paid up front.) The same is true with this book: You'll probably get excited when reading the concepts and ideas. Perhaps you'll think about how these strategies could eventually change the way you sell, and you may even take copious notes and read a few chapters several times. Then you'll put the book up on the shelf with the other sales books in your collection and go on your way.

And that is fine, IF all you want is the cotton candy buzz (and there's nothing wrong with those now and again). But if you want more than just picking up one or two ideas to add to your arsenal, I encourage you to do the following: Read a bit, put the book down, do an exercise or two, go online and explore, make a few client calls to test out a theory, then come back and read some more, and so on. Just use this book hard. I would rather you see this book as a kind of *Field Guide* that you would lug into the high country for a hike than a pristine research book that lies dormant on a shelf. Get it dirty, dog-ear the pages, rip 'em out—whatever it takes to expand your experience.

Here are some of the "added features" I've included for you to try:

• **_Exercises._** There are several exercises included in this book. Some can be done immediately, others require putting the book down and taking action in your world (such as calling clients you may have in the pipeline and having them take a specific action step). My suggestion would be to get a three-ring binder for this process, and insert three or four dividers to begin with for notes, exercises, and tools.

• **_Tools and Templates._** I will be giving you several real life examples of tools and defined processes my clients have developed over the years, along with some templates for creating these on your own. There will electronic versions of the templates at our online resource center to make it a little easier to cut and paste.

The Online Resource Center

I have created an accompanying website for readers of this book so that you'll be able not only to access "bonus features" while you're reading the book, but to provide you with several ways to stay plugged in and continue the improvement process over the long haul. You can get to the resource center by logging on to either:

http://GregBennett.blogs.com

or

www.APCProfit.com

Here is what you'll find in the resource center:

•   *Streaming Video Segments.* These feature several video interviews with myself, clients you'll read about, and salespeople and sales managers who are going through some of the same issues you are. Also included are role-plays where you'll see the strategies discussed in the book in action.

NOTE: You must have high-speed connectivity and computer speakers to view the online video segments. If you don't have high-speed connectivity, the transcripts of all video segments are available for download, or you may write our office and we will be happy to mail them to you.

•   *Tool Templates.*

•   *Blog Community.*

•   *Free Webinars.* We host regular free phone and video conferences, which you are welcome to attend and participate in. The schedule is available on the website.

•   *Contacting Me Directly.* I've always believed in being on the front lines, in the trenches, when training and coaching sales people and sales teams. I LOVE to work on specific sales issues and sales problems. So don't be afraid to e-mail me directly with questions: greg@APCProfit.com.

Remember, I succeed only when you succeed. So you and I are partners in this process. I believe teaching is more than a transfer of knowledge, a simple hand-off from me to you. I see it as more of a "merging partnership," with you and me going to work together to improve your situation (and thus mine!). Don't call me (I hate voice mail); e-mail me, and then maybe we'll chat on the phone if we need to.

Are you ready, partner?

C H A P T E R 1

Consultative Salespeople Often Struggle with Closing

As a sales trainer, coach and consultant for nearly twenty years, I've worked with hundreds of sales organizations and thousands of sales managers and salespeople, and one thing has become very apparent—many consultative salespeople, and people using consultative selling strategies, really struggle with having to push hard to "close the deal."

Consultative Selling, in a nutshell, is the art of effective questioning, listening and probing of the client to effectively ascertain their problems, challenges, goals and objectives; then presenting solution options that are customized to meet specific needs and are designed to form long-term working partnerships with the client to maximize their investment. Consultative Selling is focused almost exclusively on the client versus on the "bells and whistles" of the salesperson's product or service. The objective is to understand the client's situation to such a degree that the sale and implementation of the product or service becomes a seamless, integral part of the client's ongoing business operation. People have labeled the process of consultative selling with wonderfully creative titles like "Customer-Centered Selling" and "Value-Added Implementation." The salespeople are called "Consultative Marketing Professionals," "Implementation Specialists," and of course the old standard, "Account Executives."

No matter what name we give it, the methodology is right for the times and is the only way to professionally sell any product or service. However, there is something about this style of selling that seems to be leading to problems with getting the client to take action and closing the deal.

"My biggest challenge is getting clients to take action without coming across as pushy . . . or too salesy," said Mark DeMasse (not a real name), a top producer for a Canadian computer storage company I was consulting with a few years back. "I am definitely someone who likes to be seen as more of a consultant than a salesperson . . . but I think sometimes that hurts me because, when it is time to sell another project, or another level of service. . . . I have to get decisions, and I tend to let people off the hook because I don't want to push things too far and maybe ruin the relationship . . . and I need good relationships in order to do the work I do. If I come across as just another self-serving salesperson, we won't have the right type of relationship to work together down the road."

Mark is like many of the salespeople I've worked with, especially since the more consultative sales model came into vogue in the 1980s and 1990s: He likes the consultative selling model versus the more "traditional" pushy sales strategies, but he struggles in getting enough closed business through the pipeline. Not all salespeople are as honest and forthright as Mark, admitting his struggles with closing, many aren't even aware they have a problem, they just think this is the way sales has to be. If you want to be a consultant and not a pushy salesperson, then you have to live with clients deciding on their own, and a longer sales cycle.

Managers and business owners however can't afford to have that "just live with it" mindset; they have aggressive goals to meet and ever more demanding owners and stockholders to answer to. Managers are the ones usually contacting me, reporting that while their salespeople are competent, professional, friendly, and do a good job of knowing their clients, they aren't closing enough, fast enough to deliver the needed results.

Let's look at some of the reasons why consultative salespeople and others using consultative selling model may struggle with closing:

• *Consultative Salespeople are like the vast majority of people: They don't like conflict.* Closing typically involves some sort of conflict, where one party is asking the other party to take action of some kind. What ensues can include any or all of the following—arguments, disagreements, stalls, objections, lying, pressure, or silence. All of these are loaded with potential conflict, and conflict can lead to hurt feelings and all the negative thoughts that go with being a pushy salesperson.

Most people don't like conflict (not ALL, but most— and some people LOVE to create it). Salespeople don't like it. Clients don't like it. And we soon learn how to avoid conflict situations if at all possible. This includes the use of several degrees of lying—from subtle deception to flat-out BS in order to spare someone's feelings, or avoid a fight. It's faster, easier, and less stressful to just lie. We'll cover this in greater detail coming up when we profile the role of client in the sales situation, but for now suffice it to say we all lie to avoid conflict.

We all do it at one time or another. When you're at

your friend's house and she brings out her brand new baby for everyone to see her for the first time—and of course the poor little thing looks like the alien that attacked Sigourney Weaver—we don't let out a scream and say, "Send it back. It's not done!" No, we use some deception and say, "Ahh-hhh . . . she's so. . . . so . . . cute." Or, when you're holding a dinner party at your house and a neighbor arrives with his new girlfriend who's obviously "had some work done," you don't ask, "Wow, are you for real?" We in fact are masters of deception in these types of settings: We either pretend not to notice, or use vague terms, or just flat out lie to whatever degree necessary to avoid hurting someone's feelings, being seen as rude, or perhaps getting a punch in the nose. If we always told the truth 100 percent of the time, we probably wouldn't be very well liked.

And we don't *like* to be liked—we *love* to be liked. And in a sales situation, when we're already nervous about being too pushy, we're deathly afraid that if we cause conflict, the client won't like us (and we won't like ourselves.)

• *Consultative Salespeople are usually adamant about their dislike for traditional selling styles and the undue pressure those styles put on clients, so they over-compensate in the other direction and end up not asking for action steps.* Consultative salespeople are so anxious about being seen as "old-school" sellers that they go to great lengths to avoid putting ANY pressure on the client. They back away, won't ask for commitment. While they'll avoid the uneasiness of selling in the old-school style, they also won't get to issues that lie beneath the surface; and without issues it's very tough to solve problems, answer questions, and close deals.

• We're so paranoid about being painted with the negative brush of a sleazy salesperson, we'll subconsciously go out of our way NOT to be seen that way—meaning we won't do some of the things one MUST do to get the client to take action.

- We're thinking about this stuff all the time, and if a client should so much as mention that we're acting in that fashion, it will freak us out and make us run the other way. As in:

"Man, Tom, I've got to tell you, you're a nice guy, and we like working with you, but you're really kind of acting like a pushy salesman here." (No, no . . . not that . . . anything but . . . anything but a salesman. . . . ahhhh!!!!)

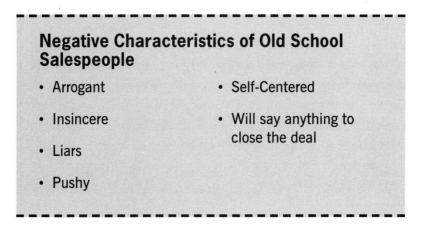

Negative Characteristics of Old School Salespeople

- Arrogant
- Insincere
- Liars
- Pushy

- Self-Centered
- Will say anything to close the deal

- *Consultative Salespeople know a good deal about the client's condition or situation, and that can lead to a greater fear on the part of the client because he knows he can't easily escape with nonaction.* This would be like going to see the doctor for a physical, and before she gets started she says: "You look like you could lose some weight, which could eventually elevate your cholesterol levels. Better watch that diet." And you say: "Sure doc. Yeah, fine. Whatever. (Now hurry, I've got a box of donuts with my name on 'em.)"

Compare that with the doctor who has already done the blood work and has the tests. And now her comment is: "Okay, your cholesterol is well over 200. You've GOT to lose some weight, and that means changing your diet." If you're the patient/client in this scenario, it's much harder to say no and avoid making changes. Which means no more donuts . . . which means pain.

While knowing a lot about the client's condition is great—and at the very heart of consultative selling—it may lead to more extreme avoidance issues on the part of the client: "Maybe I just won't get a physical at all!"

• *Consultative Salespeople forget that the "sales clock" has started and they're in a sales call playing a role, and so is the client.* Years ago I developed something I called "the sales clock," to signify the point in time during a conversation when the sales call begins and both sides slip into their roles in this human drama: one as seller, and one as buyer. And they come together in this age-old play, with one side trying to convince the other to do something, and get paid for it. And with these roles come costumes and characteristics that are inherent in that role. When the clock starts, the characters must get in their roles (whether they want to or not). The clients will act a certain way and do certain things that come with their character, and so will the sellers. Each side will also know that they are to do battle with the other character, and will instinctively do and say certain things to deal with the actions of the other.

The clock can turn on and off in an instant, with the roles suddenly being dropped and both sides returning to their former selves. Remember the old cartoon about the sheepdog and the wolf? They would ride to work together in the morning, and as soon as they clocked in all hell would break lose for they would start to play their roles— with the wolf coming up with a million different ways to get at the sheep, and the sheepdog foiling the wolf every time. Usually the sheepdog would drop the wolf off a cliff, or launch him miles away with a large catapult (they always seem to have a catapult around in the cartoons, don't they?). Then, at the end of the workday the whistle would blow, and they'd clock-out and ride home together. They'd wake up in the morning and do it all over again. The sheep-dog and the wolf would wait till the clock started before they got into character and did what they were programmed to do.

I think of a sales call in the same way, with the charac-ters of salesperson and client waiting for the "sales clock" to start before slipping into the age-old roles that have been defined over years of our collective social experience. The problem, however, is that only one of the characters is in their role: the client. The salesperson either isn't aware the clock has started, or has decided not to participate "in char-acter." Now when I say "in character," I'm not suggesting salespeople should become something they're not. I *am* say-ing they need to realize the play has started, and they're going to be seen in the role of salesperson (whether they want to act like a stereotypical one or not). Also, they must look at the person across from them as being "in character as the client."

When salespeople forget they are in a sales call, they have a tendency to see the client as a "normal human," displaying regular, socially acceptable behaviors. But they don't understand who they're messing with! We'll introduce you to this role, known as *client,* and its tendencies later on in the book.

As for the role of salesperson, some try to play it, but

without all the "messy" inconveniences, such as asking the client to take action. If you don't ask for a commitment on SOMETHING, you'll avoid all conflict in sales, but you certainly won't be successful.

     •   *Consultative Salespeople have trouble suddenly "getting into character" and becoming high-pressure closers right in the middle of the sales cycle—and they aren't familiar with other nonconfrontational closing strategies they could use instead.* Probably what I hear most from consultative salespeople is that they feel they have to change their personality in order to close a client. They only really know about the standard closing styles, and they realize they suddenly have to become more focused on "pitching" the product or on becoming creative, funny, or unbelievably motivated.

For most people, the high-pressure strategies and techniques taught with traditional selling are pretty foreign and uncomfortable. This is particularly true when salespeople are in denial about even *being* in the role to begin with: They just don't want to have to do all that ugly stuff to close a deal. ("I am NOT a salesperson . . . I am NOT a salesperson.")

There also aren't many "soft-closing" strategies available for people who don't like conflict. And those strategies that are available tend to be too complicated and aren't readily accessible in the heat of battle.

High Pressure Strategies of Old-School Sellers

- Pulling out the contract and pushing it at the client, asking them to "Push hard, third copy is yours."

- Telling a "closing story" about Ben Franklin, or a farmer with two-pigs, or any number of other analogies designed to make a point.

- Asking loaded questions that make the client feel bad: "So, do you care at all about your family?"

• *An extra reason: Consultative Salespeople, because they don't like to be in conflict situations, also tend to not have enough irons in the fire because they don't do enough prospecting (which is an activity loaded with potential conflict).* Prospecting is nearly always tied directly to closing. If you have twenty prospects who all want the one item you're selling, you don't have to be a great closer, or apply a ton of pressure. The market conditions apply the pressure. Conversely, if you can only work up the courage to prospect long enough to get five prospects into your sales pipeline, you'll have to work harder at closing the few opportunities you have: Market conditions closing *ain't gonna work.*

HARD-SELL, HIGH-PRESSURE SELLERS *COULD* CLOSE—BUT AT WHAT COST?

Make no mistake about it, as much as we despise the hard-sell techniques of "old school" sellers, they do work to get people to take action. They have techniques for applying pressure, and for brow-beating clients into a decision cause action to happen, and they do close sales.

The Hard Sell

Allow me to share a story (and we all have a story or two about hard-sell sales geeks) about a guy I knew who was selling home fire alarms, and he told me all about his closing style and how he was trained. We'll call him Wes. (No, there's no surprise ending where it's really me and I suddenly change my ways.)

"The bottom line is, if I don't put an alarm up in that house before I leave, there will be no sale," Wes said. "And I was trained to do whatever I had to do to get that alarm up on the wall, even if it meant risking a physical altercation."

To me this sounded a bit extreme, but Wes continued.

"Our pitch went like this. We would find out all we could about their family, especially the kids' names, the dog's name, the cat, everyone in the house. Then we'd do our spiel, talk about the chances for a major fire, the stats on people getting out alive, all that stuff. And the close would be asking whether they felt protecting Johnny, Jenny, and little Spot was worth the $300 set-up and $60 monthly fee."

These types of sales, and frankly this type of sales guy, have always freaked me out, mainly because he's just the epitome of everything I hate about being called a salesperson: pushy, insincere, focused on self, deceptive, fake, etc., etc. Here's how he closed:

"About midway through the call I'd pull out a contract and just start filling it out, asking how many alarms they felt they needed, and where they'd want them. A few people would stop me. If they did, I brought up the kids, how much is peace of mind worth—but most people were too afraid to say anything and would just let me go. My final move though was to just pull out one of the alarms and start screwing it in the wall. At that point, I either got a deal, or they'd be pretty upset and tell me to stop."

Wes's closing ratio was around 60 percent, but he had to deal with a good deal of conflict. I can't imagine many clients enjoying that experience and wanting to give him referrals. But in Wes's world, it's not about client's enjoying the experience, or forming long-term relationships. Wes's objective is clear: Get the client to buy on the spot.

CAN WE CREATE THE BEST OF BOTH WORLDS?

My purpose in writing this book, and the driving force behind my getting into this business to begin with, was to try and develop an approach that represented the best of both worlds: the relationship-building aspects of consultative selling, coupled with the action-oriented focus of hard-sell closing. I wanted to develop an approach to selling that at the end of the day satisfied the needs of clients, led to sales, *and* created long-term relationships.

Though combining these strategies will help both types of salespeople, I believe it will help consultative salespeople more, because I'm not sure you can teach hard-sell, me-first sellers to have a desire to form lasting relationships and focus on helping other people. Perhaps I'll be pleasantly surprised and there will be many old-school sellers who'll see the light and decide to make major changes.

Combining the Best of Both Selling Styles

Consultative Selling Positives

- Focused on the client's needs

- Fosters partnership

- Stresses long-term relationships

Hard-Close Selling Positives

- Focused on getting action

- Advancing the sale as much as possible

- More forceful, defined "asks"

Combined Qualities of Consultative Closing

- Focused on meeting clients needs, and getting them to take action

- Stressing long-term partnerships—more purposeful and direct in creating the relationship

- Always advancing the sale and closing, but positioned always as a good for the client first and foremost

LET'S START BY REDEFINING THE WORD "CLOSING"

As we explore some simple steps for improving our closing capabilities, we should start by redefining the word "closing" itself. This is a simple step, but like other steps in this book, you may find that it causes a major paradigm shift for you and how you view sales.

I've asked several groups over the years to define the word closing, and they've come back with these types of phrases:

- Getting the deal done

- Getting a YES

- Signing on the bottom line

- Getting a check

- Pushing people to decide

While these are all good descriptions, they only cover half of closing. There is another side, the NO side, or what happens if there is no deal. I teach that closing means the following:

Closing does not mean a YES decision exclusively. Closing just means "a decision." Closing can also mean a NO decision.

Old School Definition

- Closing means "YES"

Bennett's Consultative Closing Definition

- Closing means "YES" or "NO"

This distinction is critical because it elevates the other side of the equation, the NO side, to near equal status as possible answers to a question. We'll cover this in greater detail later in this book, but if we can start to gravitate to NO rather than accept MAYBE, we'll be much better off.

For when we get NO, we get reality, and when we get reality, we hear issues, and in some cases we can solve the issues and move the client back to yes.

INSTEAD OF FEARING CLOSING WE MUST LEARN TO VALUE IT AS GOOD FOR EVERYONE INVOLVED

Now that we know closing means YES or NO, we should feel better "closing the client", instead of *having* to push them into a YES or all is lost. Beyond that is the bigger issue, and one that doesn't get talked about much, which is that closing is good for the client, while *not closing* hurts the client, as well as the salespeople.

How Not Closing Hurts Clients

•   *They are stuck in their muck.* Their pains and problems still exist, and will probably get worse, because they haven't purchased the right solution (yours).

•   *The stalking process will continue.* Because clients desire to avoid conflict, they are often deceptive with their answers, especially if there is bad news to deliver. And so they hedge their words and often give salespeople false hope.

How Not Closing Hurts Salespeople

•   *We can't make money and be successful.* Enough said.

•   *We end up with clogged pipelines.* One of the biggest challenges salespeople face is clogged pipelines full of what salespeople think are potential clients, when in reality most of it is garbage that sits in there and rots.

- ***We can't help people.*** We need to either get a YES and get clients the help they need to solve problems and achieve goals, or get a NO and we can both move on to bigger and better things.

GREAT NEWS: *CONSULTATIVE CLOSING SALESPEOPLE WILL RULE THE WORLD!*

The great news for those who read this book and decide to follow my strategies to become true "Consultative Closers" is that because we will possess the deadly combo: the heart and soul of a consultative seller, with the ability to close and get people to take action. We will dominate whatever marketplace we operate in! We will create more business, develop stronger relationships, have more fun, save more clients, make more money, and generally enjoy a life in sales we can be proud of!

Closing is a good thing. Consultative Closing is an even better thing. Let's dig into the simple steps that will make you a more effective closer immediately.

REVIEW

- Consultative selling is the only way to sell, but the process can lead to problems with closing.

- Consultative salespeople typically don't acknowledge that there is a sales call taking place and that the person they're talking to is playing the role of client. This leads to an increased use of deception to avoid conflict.

• Closing needs to be redefined as not just a YES, but a YES or NO.

• Consultative salespeople typically aren't comfortable with hard-sell closing strategies, though there are some positives to the harder style, like getting people to take action.

• The secret to success in sales in the future is combining the best of consultative selling with the action mindset of harder-edge sellers (all while building and sustaining strong client relationships).

CHAPTER 2

The Role of Mini-Steps in the Closing Process

I know without a doubt that with my simple *but incredibly powerful* concepts contained in this chapter anyone can become a better closer. As the title of the book promises, these are simple steps that can be applied to any sales process within any type of sales organization, guaranteed to help you make dramatic improvements almost immediately. All you have to do is have an open mind and be willing to try.

For hundreds of years the selling process has pretty much remained the same, with a seller on one side and a client on the other. As the two parties approach, there is a distinct time before the sale, when the salesperson "owns" the product, followed by a time after the sale, when the client owns the product: a two-stage process. The selling approach itself is similar—it's always been a two-step process, where sellers approach clients and determine whether there is an interest. If so, the seller puts the client in the pipeline (or "hopper" if you will), which is step one. The seller then continues to pursue the client with repeated calls, writing proposals, chasing down multiple decision makers, etc., until the deal is sold, which is step two.

Typically all the little tasks involved in the pursuit and closing steps are generally kept hidden from the client and discussed only on the "sales side" of things (among salespeople, management, production people, and accounting). It's rare for a salesperson to share the selling, executing, and follow-up processes with the client. Salespeople typically just *do* the tasks; they don't *talk* about the tasks.

This is where my strategies come in, and I guarantee they'll change the way you pursue and close business.

MINI-STEPS

Of all the sales and sales management strategies, concepts, techniques, and ideas I've created over the years, nothing has had a greater impact on the success of my clients than the introduction of *Mini-Steps* into the consultative sales process. Basically what I'm doing with Mini-Steps is breaking down the normally hidden pursuit—closing and servicing steps involved in the sales process—into "Mini-Steps," and then sharing those steps on a time-line with the client.

This is a unorthodox approach to sales, but when done correctly in conjunction with the other key strategies I teach in this book, the results are amazing! After helping hundreds of companies and thousands of salespeople and business owners to identify and use the Mini-Step closing process, I've seen closing ratios improve, the sales cycle get shorter, client satisfaction grow, and overall sales performance attain new heights.

More on the Definition of Mini-Steps

Mini-Steps are simply identifiable steps that need to be taken by the client, the salesperson, the company, or an outside party: *before, during, and after the sale.* The steps can be internal-process oriented (e.g., filling out a credit application); creative-development oriented (e.g., a scheduling a brainstorming session with your team); follow-up oriented (e.g., a "post-buy" client review); or any other number of areas we'll discuss in greater detail.

So much of the typical two-step process (where these Mini-Steps would be typically hidden away and never discussed) involves moving forward, based on a loose verbal confirmation, or usually on an assumed consent. With our Mini-Step process, almost all the steps are going to be based on someone taking physical action—scheduling a meeting, ordering a part, penciling in something on a calendar. We'll explain the reason for this coming up later.

How Mini-Steps Differ from Merely Identifying the Sales "Process"

Nearly all of the most popular Consultative Selling training programs and systems encourage sales people to identify stages (e.g., exploratory, probing, discovery) within the sales process. What makes the Mini-Step process different is the identifying and breaking down of *specific tasks* within those stages, and in many cases, creating additional tasks that are purposely designed to achieve certain outcomes.

I developed the Mini-Steps process several years ago, but it wasn't until after I began consulting with Point B Solutions Group, LLP, a professional services firm specializing in project leadership, that I began to realize that what I'd done with Mini-Steps is basically applied the concepts of *project management to the sales process.*

As I continued to work with Point B on their sales processes and helped to expand their new business efforts, I realized why their service is so very much needed, and why Mini-Step Closing resonates so strongly with sales-people and sales managers: Whether implementing a com-plicated business system in the case of Point B, or trying to reel in a complicated sale, it's unnatural for people to break down stages into steps. For some reason most of us stop one step away from breaking down and listing the specific action steps required in a staged process. In some cases it's because we don't know the specific steps required; in other cases we know the steps, but fail to put them down on paper.

Mini-Steps

Here is a quick overview of what Mini-Steps are and what they're designed to do:

Mini-Steps Are:

- Identifiable steps within the sales process.

- Physical, action-oriented steps taken by the client, the salesperson, or a third party (e.g., internal accounting, production personnel, service reps).

- Steps we can put on a time-line of Before, During, and After the sale.

Mini-Steps Are Designed to:

- Move the closing process from the verbal to the physical, as clients will now prove how "interested" they are through their actions and not their words.

- Give the salesperson several opportunities to "take the client's temperature" during their time in the sales pipeline process. If the client won't take a simple action-oriented Mini-Step early on, it is a clear sign that something has happened inside that client's decision-making process (e.g., not getting consensus, someone has "poisoned the well," etc.).

- Show the client that the salesperson has a much more thorough process before, during, and after the sale—this will make the competition look lazy and weak in comparison.

- Remove the client from the market by tying him down to a course of action early. Once steps are taken, it is much harder to undo those steps and go in another direction.

There are no rules for how many steps there MUST be in your process, or for what steps MUST be included. The amount and scope of the steps you develop are totally up to you. I have clients who have three main steps, and others who have over thirty. *The key is to have enough of the right steps to effectively drive your sales machine.*

I've had people ask, "What's so new about this? I've known about getting buy-in for a long time." That's partially true: The concept of getting steady buy-in has been a major part of consultative selling for a long time. The main difference is that most of the "buy-in" process was done on the surface. It relied on verbal affirmation, which we know is mostly (not entirely) overly optimistic on the client's part in order to avoid conflict. Also, most of the "buy-in" process was done behind the scenes and away from the client; we were in our minds advancing the sale, but the client probably had a different interpretation of the situation. We just never really had the means to find out how they really felt—not by their verbal interpretation, but by their action or nonaction.

The Mini-Step concept is also much different from the typical action steps we may define internally when using a database management system. We can enter two or three steps associated with closing the deal, such as Make a Proposal, Get a Verbal Confirmation, or Order Approved. We then attach a percentage of close to those steps: Make a Proposal-25 percent, or Get a Verbal Confirmation-75 percent, etc. Those are fine as basic starting points, and some of them may even be included in our full sales process, but we're going to be developing a different type of action step that is more focused on the client, and is more consultative in nature.

Replacement Windows

To illustrate my point, allow me give you a tangible example from a very simple sales process I was involved with as the client, and then I will introduce you to a much more complicated, larger sales process with one of our case studies, Point B. First, let's talk replacement windows.

My wife Rosemary and I were considering putting replacement windows in our home. Because we have a pretty big, older house, we knew it was going to be a monster project. It was around September, and we were planning to have them put in just before spring: maybe February or March of the following year.

We called several window companies we'd heard about or had been referred by friends, and we had them all drag their sales kits out to our home to talk to us about buying their windows.

I don't know whether you've ever been through this process, but it's entertaining if nothing else. These folks have all sorts of cool presentation tools and gadgets to demonstrate how thick their windows are, or how well insulated and fire-retarding their windows can be (you can imagine the fire display . . . *watch your eyebrows kids*). And they ask you those questions that make you feel like such an idiot.

"So, Mr. Bennett, what's the U-factor you've got in your windows now?" the salesperson asks, assuming that everyone MUST know this stuff.

"Uh . . . 60 . . . or 70 . . . you know . . . whatever it takes," I sputter, looking at my wife, who I know is thinking, "What kind of loser am I married to that doesn't know our U-factors?"

"Well, typically it's never more than a point 1," the seller says, laughing to himself I'm sure, thinking, "*60 or 70*—what a moron."

So we go through these various sales presentations, and then we come to the end, when someone has to do something. And because no one seems to have a logical plan for how this is supposed to go, these salespeople ask us: "What do you want to do next?"

Hell, I don't know. I don't even know what my U-factor is and you want *me* to tell you what we're supposed to do next? Why do salespeople always ask that question of clients? Clients aren't the expert—the salesperson is the expert. That's like the doctor asking the patient, "So, what tests do you want to run next?"

Anyway, back to windows. All the salespeople from all the window companies pretty much had the same process (the typical two-step process):

- They asked if we're ready to go now. We said no, not until spring.

- They all said, "Okay, we'll wait to hear from you when you've interviewed the other companies and have decided."
- There were no next steps, no process for deciding, nothing.
- There were two steps in the pipeline: We enter into the pipeline and maybe we come out of the pipeline.

I would imagine all of these salespeople ran back to their offices, entered "The Bennetts" into their pipelines, and probably put us down for "90 percent chance of close in February or March." And I can imagine several managers asking, "You think we'll get the Bennetts?" and the salespeople answering, "Oh yeah, they seemed very interested. Plus, they're pretty clueless. I mean, that Mr. Bennett thinks he has an U-factor of 60 or 70!!!" Everyone has a good laugh as they high-five each other and put our name up on the board as "done!" Ding. . . . ding . . . ding. *Wally, the window sales guy, may get the first-quarter trip to Vegas.*

Of course, what these guys don't see is that the situation is much different from our perspective: *We don't know enough to even ask intelligent questions!!* We're waiting for *someone* to have a process—a system—for helping us make the right choice. We don't know any better. We don't trust salespeople (because we're clients), and we don't trust our own judgment. And yet everyone of these salespeople is just assuming we're going to be able to recognize the differences in companies and products, and give them the business six months from the first call.

The only steps any of them suggested were things like, "I'll call you in a few months and see where you are, okay?" or "When the new catalogues arrive, I'll send them over, sound good?" Yeah, sure . . . great, whatever.

Another thing these guys missed, and we all do it so I'm not pointing them out specifically, is that our thinking about windows is probably priority #100 in our busy lives of work, and family, and kids activities, and church, etc., but to the salespeople involved, our windows are priority #1. What they don't see is that the minute they leave, we stop thinking about windows, as the rest of our life comes barging in. If someone doesn't force our hand, and just waits for us to get around to making a decision, that "February or March" may turn into *April or May* . . . then *May or June* . . . then maybe *end of the summer* . . . then on to fall . . . winter . . . spring . . . and so on.

Now let's look at how the introduction of Mini-Step Closing would change *everything.* Instead of having just two steps in the process—*enter and exit the pipeline*—the window company comes up with the following Mini-Steps (and these should give you a better understanding of what the steps are and how they can work):

- Schedule meeting for free visit from company designer

- Get credit application (if funding through company)

- Schedule walk-through with installers
- Reserve windows from factory
- Set meeting to do a client walk-through of factory

These are just a few examples. In reality there might be more or less; again—how many you have doesn't matter. But watch how they change the end of the sales call.

The salesperson shows us a time-line on a large, long sheet of paper. "Well, Mr. and Ms. Bennett, we're a little different from most other window companies in that we have a pretty thorough process before and after you purchase. Let me show you. Since we're here in September and you're looking to get started in February or March, first thing we need to do is pick a tentative install date—when we can target getting started."

We'll get into this more later, but picking an install date, or what I call a "closing date," is the first step to developing a "closing plan." When we pick a closing date we move from "thinking about doing something in February or March" (which, as we've demonstrated, could easily drift to summer, then fall) to a more concrete plan for turning this desire or *wish* into a reality.

The salesperson continues, "Okay, so let's say that March 1 is the date . . ."

(Even if I argue) "Well, that's not for certain," I reply.

"No problem. It's just for planning purposes. So what we need to do now is schedule a few things in our early stages of discovery, like this initial one of scheduling a free meeting with our design team."

"Well, I'm not sure if I'm going to go with you guys quite yet," I say, afraid I might be making a decision.

"Oh, no problem, I realize that. You aren't obligated to anything, in fact this visit will help you whether you go with us or not. How does late next week look?"

The minute I start penciling in dates with this guy, the closer he is to taking me off the market and moving toward new windows with an install date of March 1st. It's also going to dramatically highlight the difference between his company and all the others. Can you imagine the look on the next window seller's face when I ask, "So, where are the steps in your discovery process?" and "When can we schedule the factory walk-through?"

"Uh. . . . what?"

SOME TRUTHS YOU NEED TO KNOW ABOUT CLIENTS

One of the first insights I try to share in workshops is that we are generally clueless about the *other side* in the sales situation. We just have no idea what we're up against when we're dealing with a client when the "sales clock" is on. No idea.

When we focus on "improving our closing," we have a tendency to work on *our* closing skills: How can I improve what I'm saying, or doing? Are there better ways I should be presenting? Should I be getting different people in the room? and so on. Again, there is nothing necessarily wrong with improving in these areas, they're just not as important as understanding the client's mindset and tendencies.

Once you really understand how clients are likely to act in certain situations, and how they're likely to think and respond, you'll have a tremendous advantage. Just like in football, good players and coaches know that to win you have to focus not only on what you're doing, but also on what the other team is likely to do in different situations.

Remember the movie a few years back called *What Women Want,* with Mel Gibson? It was about an advertising executive who took a knock on the head, and when he came around he could suddenly hear the internal thoughts of women who were nearby. He could hear women in stores, at the office, at home. If you've seen the movie, you know that Mel's character soon realized that a) he was surprised to hear what women had to say about him, b) he was shocked at how his actions affected them, and c) he could use this "gift" to manipulate work situations to give him an advantage.

Can you imagine our reaction if we could hear the internal thoughts of our clients as we're going through the selling and closing process? We might be as shocked as Mel's character in the movie. Let's imagine for a moment that we are watching a typical sales interaction, and we'll magically be able to read Bob, our client's, brainwaves *(in italics)* as he deals with a salesperson:

• The salesperson walks in and shakes hands with Bob the client.

> Bob thinks: *"This guy is nervous, his hands are all sweaty. Man, I HOPE that was sweat."*

• Salesperson starts to ask him about his business: "How are things going, Bob?"

> Bob thinks: *"How long is this going to take? Do I tell him business is a little off? Nooooo . . . he'll get all excited and start pitching me."*

> Bob says: "Things are going pretty well, I'd say."

• Salesperson mentions one of his features and benefits: "Bob, as you can see, according to the *Business Journal,* we're the top rated financial assessment firm in the city and have been for five years running."

Bob thinks: *"So what. I don't buy into those bogus lists, they've screwed us every year when we should have been in the top five."*

Bob says, "Really? That's interesting."

• Salesperson moves into a closing stage: "Bob, I'd like to get started working on your project. Can we get the go ahead today?"

Bob thinks: *"Are you nuts? No way. Think . . . think . . . need an escape. Come on, Bob. Oh, got it."*

Bob says: "Well, let me do this. I'd like to think about it a bit more."

• Salesperson presses on: "Okay. Well, what are *your* general thoughts? Do you like our solution option?"

Bob thinks: *"I can't stand this "solution option" or this guy. How can I get rid of him? Come on, Bobby, think, man."*

Bob says: "Well, I like a lot of it. I just have to think about it a bit more. Tell you what, can you work up a few different options for us to look at, maybe with some different price points?"

• Salesperson, pleased with the positive response, says: "Sure . . . ," and off he goes to do more work on a client he thinks is positive, but who in reality is anything BUT.

SOME FRIGHTENING THINGS CLIENTS DO IN THEIR ROLE

As we can see from reading the client's internal dialogue, clients often think and act differently than they really feel.

While we all do this from time to time, this is particularly troubling because we're basing so much of our advancement in the sales process on what the client says (not to mention that we have to make a living dealing with these guys).

Here are some other characteristics that come along with the client role:

• **Clients lie to whatever degree is needed in order to avoid conflict.** AND THEY DON'T EVEN THINK OF IT AS LYING AT THE TIME. These lies will range from slight deception like, "I'll take a look at it . . ." to flat out lying, "I talked to a few other people and they weren't crazy about it."

The example I like to give is from our family's dinner table, when the telemarketing folks would call just as you were sitting down. My favorite deceptive escape always was, "I'm sorry . . . we're moving to Seattle." My youngest daughter, who was around 5 at the time, would say, "But Dad . . . that's a lie."

"Well, it's not really a lie . . . it's uh . . . well. . . ." I couldn't really explain that the "sales clock" was on, and that within my character role as client I could suddenly lie with ease.

• **They love to act more interested than they really are.** This is probably the #1 escape route of clients in the sales process. They know that salespeople desperately want to hear good news, even if it's all made up, so they'll feign interest knowing it will get rid of salespeople, and keep everyone feeling "okay" as the process moves along.

• **When they think NO, they say "MAYBE."** This is the standard modus operandi for clients. It is really at the heart of stalled sales, because it's the exact opposite of the way salespeople interpret: *salespeople hear "MAYBE" and think YES* (much more on this coming up).

The nicer you are, the harder you work to serve the client, and the more they may lie. If a salesperson is a jerk, I don't mind telling him to go pound sand. But if the person is nice—and they've done everything I've asked, and they've taken me to dinner or a ball game—well, then it's much tougher to tell them the ugly truth. I'd rather just stall, or blame it on someone else.

I remember a situation where a friend of mine had referred a woman to me who had left the corporate world and had decided to open up her own newsletter design business. At the time I was interested in possibly doing a newsletter, and so it made sense to have her come in. Well, her newsletters were not so good; in fact, they were terrible. But did I say that? Of course not. I gave her false hope in order to remove conflict: "I'm fairly interested, I think. Why don't you work up some examples and let me take a look?"

She was so nice, and was trying so hard to get this new business launched, what was I going to do, tell her the ugly truth? Please. It would have crushed her. So instead I did the "noble thing" by giving her some false hope, and by having her waste time designing more bad newsletters I'll never buy.

I understand that some of us don't like to see other people in this light, or perhaps you don't lie *ever,* even a little. And that's fine, but we're talking about the majority of people we're going to encounter in a day.

CLIENTS AND THE CLOSING PROCESS

Since we're doing a pretty thorough review of the "other side" in our sales play, we need to talk about how clients act during closing. Because most people operate from the old two-step process with only one big step to close on, the pressure can be enormous. And with increased pressure, their evasive and deceptive techniques will become even more amplified and extreme.

Here is some sample deceptive closing dialogue between client and salesperson:

SALESPERSON: "So what do you think, Anne? Are we ready to move ahead?"

CLIENT (thinking *NO,* but saying): "Well, I think we might be a bit closer. I'd like to talk with a few other folks here."

SALESPERSON (thinking: *Good, good*): "Okay. Well, do you think we could get started on this right away?"

CLIENT (still thinking *NO,* but searching for a positive escape): "Tell you what. If you could do me a favor, I'd like to have you do a bit more work on the overall proposal, and then come back and show it to my supervisor. I'm sure he'll probably be pretty positive about it.

SALESPERSON (thinking: *Well, that's not great, but I can't give up on this, I've got too much invested*): "Oh, well, yeah, I guess I could do that, as long as you're saying you're still interested."

CLIENT (thinking: *This is a piece of cake. It's easy to be INTERESTED. I'm interested in going to Mars next week too.*): "Oh yeah, I'm VERY interested in . . . you know . . . eventually doing something."

THE CLIENT'S STALLING LANGUAGE TOOL BOX

We may not realize it, but we're all "gifted" with deceptive language skills. And we somehow know how to use these skills when we're forced into potential conflict situations, such as being a client in a sales call. As you can see in this table below, there can be quite a "reality disconnect" between what we think and what we say—all to avoid conflict:

Client Thinks	Client Says
I don't believe what he's saying	Wow . . . really?
I'm not excited at all	Interested
I will never buy	May end up doing something
I'm throwing it in the trash	I'll pass this around
I'm going to forget you were here	Let me think about it a bit
I'll NEVER call you	I'll try to get in touch with you
NO	Maybe
	I'll strongly consider it
	I'll give it some *real* thought (versus??)
	I like a lot of it
	We may do something later

As we touched on earlier, the only reason clients can get away with this behavior—of not taking action and just pretending to be "interested"—is because *salespeople allow them to*. In fact, salespeople not only allow them to act this way, they WANT and NEED them to act this way.

See, here is the real sick issue: Salespeople and deceptive clients are *co-dependent,* if you will, in this sick "circle of death." You've got one side, the client, pretending to be "interested" mainly to avoid conflict. The other side, the salesperson, accepts the pretend "interested" answer without challenge, because they too don't like conflict, and they want a full pipeline of prospective clients (mainly so they don't have to go out and find new ones!).

Clients lie and salespeople are fine with it. They both get their needs met—on the surface. Just like any addict and his supplier, the immediate high may be fine for both, but the end result is destructive.

This dysfunctional little dance is quite destructive in the end: Clients don't get their needs met (because they never commit to getting better); salespeople can't close; sales managers can't count on projections; top management can't count on hitting overall sales numbers; and companies can't survive and thrive.

MINI-STEPS ARE ALL ABOUT ACTION VS. VERBAL

> What you're doing speaks so loudly I can't hear what you're saying.
>
> **—Anonymous**

I've always loved this adage because it hits the nail on the head when describing the problems consultative salespeople suffer from when attempting to close: *They rely almost entirely on what clients say versus what they actually do (or don't do).*

So many of our problems in sales and closing (and in dealing with deceptive clients) are caused by our insistence on relying on the spoken word versus physical action when assessing where someone may or may not be in the closing process. We totally rely on verbal "commitments" when assessing where an opportunity may be within the sales process.

I can't tell you how many hundreds of times I've heard something like this from salespeople when talking about an opportunity:

> "So, what is happening with the ABC Account?" I ask.
>
> "It looks pretty good. I mean, Tom, my main guy over there, has *said* it looks like something they'll end up doing," the seller says as he gleefully adds ABC to his ever-growing list of clients in his imaginary pipeline.
>
> "So you wrote up the initial agreement?" I ask, even though I can guess at what's coming.
>
> "Well, not yet, but he *said* he didn't see any real problems in getting that done next week. And he *also mentioned* that they'd *probably* get started with the full roll out sometime next month, *assuming* everything is okay with upper management," he says proudly.
>
> "Okay. When is he presenting to upper management?"
>
> "He *said* he *wanted to* get it up there later this week," now annoyed that I would DARE probe into this *done deal.*

Perhaps this deal will still get done—perhaps. But in more cases than not, these verbal commitments end up falling apart, or getting hung up, or stalled. Salespeople just don't take into account the gifted deceptive artists they're messing with during a sales call.

Are some "Aha lights" starting to go on for you now? Are you seeing that you're probably operating in a similar situation as the window salesmen we met? Are you out there doing your own version of the ol' two step process? Oh sure, you may have a more complicated product, and may have identified some buy-in points along the way, but if you're like most salespeople, you haven't taken the time to purposely write down, and even develop, several Mini-Steps that you can share with the client.

There are several commonalities that go with having essentially a two-step process:

- Clients usually don't know what is supposed to happen in the sales process, so they follow the salesperson's lead. If the seller won't lead, then their instinct tells them to wait to make decisions.

- Most of the tasks involved between steps one and two are never shared or talked about with the client. They're just done behind the scenes.

- Almost all advancement is handled verbally, with salespeople asking clients vague questions like, "How do you feel?" or "How does that sound?" or "Are you guys interested?" And clients respond with equally vague answers like, "Maybe," or "We might be," or "It looks pretty interesting."

- There are rarely firm time-lines that go with a sales process. Clients talk in generalities, such as, "We'd like to do something fairly soon," "I'd say by spring, or early summer," or "Later this year, maybe in early fourth quarter."

When you break a two-step process down into Mini-Steps, you accomplish several positive things: Mainly you create multiple opportunities to close the client on action steps, enabling you to get a more accurate reading of whether the sale is still on track or not.

REVIEW

- For hundreds of years, selling has been a basic two-step process, with a seller on one side and a client on the other. Step one was before the sale, as salespeople tried to move the client toward step two, which was some sort of ending, with a client saying yes, or just drifting away.

- We're revolutionizing the way salespeople approach sales by turning the two-step process into a multi-step process we call Mini-Steps.

- Mini-Steps are identifiable, action-oriented steps that need to be taken by the client, the salesperson, the company, or an outside party—before, during, and after the sale.

- There are many benefits that come from developing Mini-Steps. The main one is in getting action or nonaction from a client, versus the normal verbal confirmation, which often is deceptive in its positive tone

- When clients are in their role and the sales clock is on, they can use a great deal of deception to avoid conflict. They often act more interested than they really are, which can confuse salespeople (especially when salespeople are desperate to hear good things).

Bonus Materials Available at the Online Resource Center:

• A video streamed message from me on the deceptive nature of clients and salespeople when the sales call is in progress.

• An MP3 audio download and a written transcript of the same message are also available at the Online Center.

CHAPTER 3

How to Create Mini-Steps in the Closing Process

As we approach creating Mini-Steps and learning how to use them in our closing process, we need to keep a few important overall themes in mind. First of all, Mini-Step Closing will certainly be good for us, the salespeople, because it will lead to more closing, and faster closing. However, *Mini-Steps are really designed to be a much better process for clients* who generally HATE going through the buying and closing involved in a sale.

HELP THE CLIENT MAKE BETTER DECISIONS: CREATE A DISCOVERY QUESTIONNAIRE

I think we as salespeople become way too "inside" our own worlds, and assume that clients are more knowledgeable then they really are. We assume they know everything about their "condition": their problems, challenges, and needs. We assume they know about our industry and market. We assume they know everything about our products, and our competitor's products, and the differences between them. And we assume they know enough about all this to make the right decision on the right "fix" for their situation. There are a few clients who do, but most clients are too focused inside their own worlds to have time keeping up to speed on ours.

An analogy I like to use here is the relationship between a doctor and a patient. Can you imagine a doctor "selling" the way many salespeople do, making gross and dangerous assumptions that patients know what they're doing?

> *Hi Greg, I'm Doctor Hicklin. How are you? Listen, I'm going to assume you know what's going on with you, and that you know all about what I've got here. So I'm going to just wheel it all out so you can decide what you want to do. Okay, let's see, these are all the pills I could prescribe, and here's some of our gauzes and bandages, those are pretty cool. Oh, and over here—you'll love this stuff—we've got all our heavy equipment. This one here will x-ray the hell out of you. Oh, and this one is our new MRI machine. Okay, so what do you want to do? If you have any questions, just let me know.*

I've had this experience more times than I care to remember as a client trying to buy something, especially (and ironically I might add) with the more complicated, expensive items, like computers, cars, or even property.

I remember a few years back my wife and I were contemplating buying some mountain property here in Colorado, where we hoped to build a log cabin. Now I may be a native Coloradoan, but that doesn't mean I know squat about buying mountain property, or building a cabin. Both my wife and I were pretty much clueless about the process. We didn't know the value of property; we didn't know how to start the cabin-building process; we didn't know what we should look out for. We didn't even know how much we didn't know.

And yet when we started the process with a cabin-building company, or a real estate development company, they would always be asking us, *"What do you guys want to do?"*

"Well, buy some land. Maybe build a cabin?" I'd answer, trying not to look like the clueless dolt I truly was.

Then the questions would come: "What type of land do you want?" "How much are you looking to spend?" "What type of cabin are you looking to build?" "What are you going to do about water and power?"

I don't know . . . I don't know . . . I DON'T KNOW!

Salespeople don't realize just how stupid they can make clients feel, usually without meaning to, just through assuming clients know more than they do (remember my U-factor answer?). And because I'm clueless as a client, I feel at a total disadvantage and vulnerable with a salesperson who obviously knows more than I do. This often leads to procrastination, indecision, and eventually stalled, or lost, sales.

When buying that cabin we needed just ONE person to have a process to help us know what we should be thinking about and what to compare, and educating us on the various problems to avoid. Again, no one I've ever come across has processes, but if they did, here is what it *could have* sounded like:

"Well, Mr. and Ms. Bennett, you said you're just in the exploratory phases, and that's great. We deal

with lots of folks just like you, and what we have is a thorough process of discovery we go through to help you decide what you should be thinking about and comparing. Even if you end up never using our company, at least you'll feel better about the decisions you make in the future. The first thing we have is this short exploratory questionnaire to help you determine the general direction of your possible project. Then we should at least schedule a meeting with what we call our "dream design team." Again, no obligation at all. Meeting with these folks will help you decide if you even want to pursue the project. How does that sound?"

Doesn't that sound much more professional, and thorough, and totally customer-centered and *consultative?* It's consultative closing and it's designed to make me, the client, feel smarter, more in control.

Now can you imagine how hard it would be for us to go with another firm once we've started down this path? Especially if I talk to their competitors and none of them have anything even close. This is one example of how Mini-Step Closing will separate you from the competition.

By helping the client make better decisions you will make them feel smarter, more informed, and they'll like you for it. When clients like you, they have a tendency to trust you. And when they trust you, they'll go through the closing process much faster, and end up being long-term clients who will refer tons of business your way.

MAXIMIZE THEIR INVESTMENT: OFFER IMPLEMENTATION SERVICES

Another area we assume clients know more than they do is in the implementation of our product or service. We assume they know what they're doing when they take their new toy home. In many cases they're even more clueless after they own the thing, which is exactly when they're most excited about using it!

As we'll see in Chapter 6, we as salespeople have a tendency to take the sale to the ocean's edge then push the client out to sea, assuming they know how to navigate.

The Mini-Steps you'll be creating not only help the client make decisions BEFORE they own the product, but will help them maximize their investment after the sale. Also in Chapter 6, we'll get into the specifics of what these "After-Sales Steps" could be, but an example would be offering a free "add on" service 90 days after installation.

Let's go back to the example of me buying a cabin. A post-buy Mini-Step could be an add-on element of our choice, 60 or 90 days after the cabin is done:

"One extra touch we offer Mr. and Ms. Bennett is a complimentary add-on feature 60 days after the cabin is done. You have a choice of a free barbecue pit, custom window boxes, or a nice stand-alone wooden swing. Even though you haven't officially decided to go with our firm, IF YOU WERE to go with us, which one would you most likely go with?"

By having this "add-on" feature, the cabin-building firm accomplishes several things:

• The builder helps me, the cabin owner, maximize my investment by adding on a functional little element that helps me enjoy the cabin that much more.

• As mentioned before, this step separates the builder from the competitors, who would just as soon never hear from the homeowner again because it means "problems."

- The builder gets me, the cabin buyer, into a "post-buy" mindset, where I'm already envisioning the cabin being built, and seeing their firm doing work with me down the road. Those are powerful images for a buyer to be seeing early on in the sales process.

Again, we can see that Mini-Step Closing is all about forming better relationships with clients. Even as we're "closing them," it just won't feel like closing, which is one of the main goals of my process.

THE DIFFERENT TYPES OF MINI-STEPS

Mini-Steps aren't *just* a series of things, or tasks, we need to do as salespeople in order to "complete an order," such as turning in paperwork, submitting credit applications, or recording the sale in the database. These tasks are indeed one type of Mini-Step "To-Do's," as described below, but there are many more we need to develop.

> Mini-Steps should be action oriented and not verbal. The action can be generated by either the salesperson, the client, an internal person (for example, bookkeeper or warehouse manager), or an external person.

Not all Mini-Steps are going to be shown to the client, or even discussed, but they're still useful in helping us determine where opportunities truly are in our pipeline.

Every salesperson or sales organization should have Mini-Steps, but how many steps and how extensive they should be depends a great deal on what you're selling and the nature of your sales process (easy or complicated, quick or time consuming, or small or large dollar commitment). I suggest beginning by creating your actual Mini-Steps in each of the following categories. Write each one on an index card. Later in the chapter we'll go over how to lay them out in a time-line for Before, During, and After the sale.

Mini-Step "To-Do's"

These are the "nuts and bolts" tasks you need to do to process an order. *Many of these steps may never be shared with the client,* but will be used by salespeople, and sales management, to see where clients truly are in the process. Think about your process and fill out a card for every one. We can revisit them later and decide which ones to keep.

Some Examples of To-Do Tasks

- Turning in an order form
- Turning in a request for quote from your production department
- Processing a credit application
- Secure the credit card down payment
- Create a production schedule
- Order materials
- Set up a delivery schedule

Questions to Ask Yourself to Help Develop These Steps

- What are tasks we have in place to assess a client's situation?

- How do we handle payment and extend credit?

- What do we need to do to order product?

- What do we need to do to schedule installation?

Mini-Steps That Help the Clients Make a Good Decision

These are steps you probably don't have in place right now, and if you do they're probably just informal things you've done without really thinking about it or calling them "steps." So it is going to take some thinking and brain-storming for you to come up with some steps.

- Think about meetings you could arrange with people on your end that could help the client make a decision. For instance, if you are selling health club memberships, and you wanted to help the client make a decision about getting started on a program, you could have a Mini-Step where they schedule a meeting with your on-site nutritionist who could give them an idea of how much weight they could lose safely over a certain amount of time. One of the things people are afraid of when looking to introduce Mini-Step Closing to their process is that these steps will make closing take too long, or will make it too complicated. I'll address this in greater detail coming up in the FAQ section at the end of this chapter. In short, however, I tell people that these steps can happen quickly, and that several can actually be done in a row or simultaneously. For instance, you could bring the nutritionist in right then for a quick interview, or you could have the nutritionist come up with a check-list for the client to review and make the assessment self-guided.

• Think about meetings you could have with others in the client's business that may help shed some light on whether your solution is a fit. Clients really appreciate any work you put into the analysis process before even coming up with your recommendation.

For clients who feel intimidated by their lack of product knowledge, these are wonderful steps to develop. It's important to keep in mind that the outcome of taking these steps may lead the client to buy from someone else, and that's just a chance we have to take. In fact, when I've helped clients come to the conclusion to buy someone else's training, I usually end up in a better, more trusting long-term relationship where they end up referring other business to me. They appreciate the honesty and my willingness to put their needs above my own. Just think if I had ignored their needs and pressed them into buying my service, even it wasn't a good fit. Yes, I'd have my one-night-stand, but it would destroy any hopes for a long-term relationship. Remember, unhappy clients tell ten people, while happy clients tell about three or four.

Examples of Steps to Help Clients Make Good Decisions

• ***ABC Telephony Services Firm.*** Schedule a meeting with ABC's IT system integration specialist to make sure all systems are compatible.

• ***XYZ Office Furniture Firm.*** Schedule a meeting with Axis's office space designers to get a free space assessment.

• ***Hot FM Radio Station.*** Schedule a meeting with the station's creative director to get some feedback on whether the client's product will translate well on radio.

- *123 Cosmetic Surgery.* Schedule a meeting with 123's computer rendering associate to give the client an opportunity to see what could be a possible outcome.

Questions to Ask Yourself to Help Develop These Steps

- Who within your office should the client talk to as they consider buying a product or service like yours (not NECESSARILY whether to buy *your* particular solution).

- Are there people involved in building the product, or installing the product, or implementing the product who should talk with the client as they're shopping?

- Are there people who could help the client see a possible outcome (e.g., a cosmetic surgeon's computer rendering).

Mini-Steps to Secure Inventory, Production, or Delivery Times

Consultative Closing is always done with the client's best interest in mind. When we have this mindset it's easier to be firm with our *ask,* because we know it's good for the client to close. By *not closing* they may not be getting the best value for their dollar.

These steps have to do with locking down space, inventory, time, materials, location, and so forth. This doesn't work in all businesses, but generally the earlier a client commits, the better. Even if you're in a business where the product or service that is delivered will be exactly the same no matter when the client commits, there may be a difference in follow-up service or which added features apply. If you don't have anything like this in place, you may consider creating a "commit early" advantage. It could be a discount on follow-up products or services, or an added-bonus of more service, or little extras if they commit by a certain time.

We want to make sure we're being truthful and not making up idle threats with these steps. For instance, suppose you sell seminar seats and you tell potential clients, "My suggestion is you commit early in order to get the $100 discount off the price at the door." The client commits, but when he shows up he finds out that everyone is getting the same $100 discount at the door. Again, why create more one-time-only, upset clients?

I like to use the concept of "penciling in," or putting things on "temporary hold," or adding people to a "priority line." These can be good for clients and get them off the fence. Again, you shouldn't make these things up if they're not real, or you have no intention of going by the priority system you've established.

Examples of Steps to Help Secure Inventory

- Penciling-in dates for a training date. (This is what I like to do with potential clients early on, whether we end up holding those dates or not, and I will give priority to clients who go through this process before others.)

- Developing a priority list for a hot item or certain types of materials.

- Taking refundable or nonrefundable deposits to hold a client's order.

- Pre-booking a set amount of products or services for future use.

Questions to Ask Yourself to Help Develop These Steps:

- What are the pre-booking advantages we have now? If there are none, are there added services or discounts we could introduce?

- Do we have a deposit system (refundable or non-refundable) in place? If not, should we develop one?

- Do we currently have a "temporary hold" policy in place? If not, would it make sense to develop one?

Mini-Steps to Help Fulfill the Order

These are the steps required to execute the order, do the work, or complete the task. Depending on the industry and how complicated your product or solution tends to be, you may have a few or many steps involved in the production process.

Several of these steps may be seen as routine, or "just part of the process," and they may well be—to us. To clients, however, our internal steps probably aren't as obvious, and knowing them may actually give clients a better appreciation for all you do to complete an order.

I think it's good to emphasize the steps within our fulfillment process that directly impact clients. For instance, in the radio industry, which is where I spent ten years of my early career in advertising sales, part of the fulfillment process included creating a radio ad. Now to radio salespeople and radio production people, creating an ad is no big deal; in fact, I knew salespeople who used to claim they could *create a 60-second ad in 60 seconds!*

Clients didn't want to hear this. To them, the creation of their radio ad was special. They imagined brainstorming sessions with creative people, announcers mulling over the copy with producers, elaborate studios with music and sound effects, etc. In reality, of course, the process isn't nearly that glamorous, but it also didn't have to be as basic as *I can create a 60-second ad in 60 seconds.* I found that by simply naming the various steps within the radio production process, and by *creating* a few more, I was able to give the clients more of what they were expecting in the process. I don't mean by *creating* steps that I made them up in name only and never actually did them. I mean that I just gave a name to a normal process, then expanded and explained it a little, and it became a separate step.

An interesting discovery I made in this process—and it's one of many little extra positives I've learned about developing Mini-Steps—is that *highlighting and expanding the various steps within the process to create your product or service (in my case it was radio ads), actually made the product better!* When I told the client that we now had an official "brainstorming session" with the station's creative team, it was a tangible step that clients liked to hear about, and one that matched some of what they imagined the process to be. Not only that, but when we did it, the outcome was a better radio ad! I would imagine this same dynamic would apply to almost any business: When you focus on how you do what you do to create a better end product, it's bound to improve.

Some Examples

- Steps that highlight the "inside production" elements of what you produce

- Any special production elements you may have, especially ones that separate you from the competition

Questions to Ask Yourself to Help Develop These Steps

- Does your normal product development process lend itself to a tour, or special inside participation?

- Are there special elements you can develop or create that no one else is doing, and can you find a way to invite the client in to participate?

Mini-Step Special Events for Clients

An interesting step I've introduced to several clients is an invitation to some sort of business or social outing. This step works particularly well with longer-term sales cycles, but can still be effective with more transactional, quick-turn sales. The concept is not only to get the client to take action on something (which is an important point of all Mini-Steps), but to *add value to the relationship.*

Types of Events

- ***Industry Workshops and Seminars in Your Area.*** Get a calendar of interesting events coming up. You can use these opportunities to invite clients to accompany you, or perhaps send them as your guest.

- ***Networking Events.*** Clients also need to generate sales and are usually appreciative of salespeople who give them referrals that can generate new business.

- ***Roundtable Discussions You Facilitate.*** Even if there are no meetings or events coming up in your area, why not put on your own? I call these meetings roundtable discussions and they can be as simple as inviting two or three clients to a breakfast meeting, to as elaborate as a weekend retreat in the mountains.

ESTABLISHING A TIME-LINE

Once we've listed the steps that apply to our situation we need to lay them out in loose order: Before, During, and

After the sale. I'd suggest using index cards for each step so you can easily move them around. It's okay if some of the steps happen concurrently, or if you aren't sure which step should come first: They don't have to be in strict order.

Now establish a fictitious start date of an order. Finally, next to each step working back from the start date, put a time frame next to the action step. For instance if you have a step to secure an exclusive piece of inventory, should it be finalized 60 days before the start date? 40 days? 20 days? If there is no hard rule or deadline on a particular step, just write down an estimated time.

It's important to point out right here that just because you have multiple steps, and suggested time frames listed for those steps, doesn't always mean you are locked into those time frames. For example, if you've listed a brainstorming meeting with your creative team as something that could happen 30 days before the start date, you don't have to wait 30 days before you hold the meeting: You could radically speed everything up and have the meeting the next day, or even that afternoon. The deadlines and time frames of the Mini-Steps can either be suggested periods of times, or hard and fast rules, depending your particular product or service. A hard-and-fast-rule example would be in the mortgage refinance business, where there is a 72-hour right of rescission law in place that requires that time period before moving forward.

Another side benefit of Mini-Step Closing (and there ARE a lot of side benefits) is that you can attach action dates to just about any time length required in the sales process. That applies whether that time length is the amount of time required for the sale of a very complicated product, or it's just a client saying, "We're not going to be doing anything for at least another six months."

Now instead of just going away and coming back in six

months, you can pull out our handy Mini-Step Time-Line Planner and start to give dates to tasks. As you begin to attach dates to tasks, you might say, "Okay, Mr. Client, if you ARE serious about six months, we'd better start the planning process now." We'll get into using Mini-Steps to close in greater detail in Chapter 4, but when you have several steps *between here and there* you are able not only to force the client to tell you whether he's serious about doing something in six months, but you'll take him "off the streets" and away from competitors if he really is serious.

THE REASON FOR THE "START DATE" OR "CLOSING DATE"

My wife and I have purchased a few houses over the years, and I always found it interesting to observe what happens when you establish a "closing date" for signing the mortgage. Up to that point, everything sort of exists in a world of "promise and make believe." You're making offers and counter offers, exchanging commitments, and supplying information, and then suddenly your realtor says, "Okay, we've set the closing date for December 2." Once that date is established, everything begins to move from the ethereal mist of knowing we're going to need to get something together at some point, to the hard reality of having to get it all together by a certain date. And as that date approaches, everyone is scurrying around knowing this impending date is on the calendar.

Here is how this process sounds:

SALESPERSON: "What we need to do now, Mr. Client, is pick a tentative Start Date for this project."

Or:

> SALESPERSON: "What I recommend now, Mr. Client, is picking a date we'll target as the Commitment Date."

Whether you call it a Commitment Date, or a Start Date, or any other name, it really doesn't matter as long as you establish that this is the date we'll be targeting to get started, sign the deal, hand over the merchandise, or begin the service—whatever applies to your particular situation.

I've applied the same principle to the sales process, and the same focused attention applies and things get done. Here are some of the reasons why establishing a "Start Date" or "Closing Date" is effective within Mini-Step Closing:

•   As soon as you pick a Start Date you begin to give form to this "pretend future world" of loose thoughts and ideas about possibly doing something at some future point in time—maybe. Clients often say things like, "Well, I think we'd like to do something at some point." Then they list some loose time frame (remember us with our storm windows?), such as spring time, this winter, early next year, or sometime over the next six months. The problem, of course, is we don't know how much of that is real. Are they really going to "do something"? If so, is it really going to be "early next year"? Because we're living in a "pretend future world" those dates can start to drift: This winter can become next spring, then next summer, then next fall, etc.

•   With a date picked, whether that date is tomorrow or two years from now, you can start to look at your list of Mini-Steps. Backing up from the start date, you can give those steps dates as well, and when you have dates attached to tasks, you are more likely to get action—or nonaction. This means, of course, that with a date attached to an action step it's going to lead to an ASK, and an ASK will lead to closing for an answer: either YES or NO.

•   Even if the client can't or won't give you a closing date, you should still develop one on your own. This will work to at least get the process started and help turn it from a "pretend date" and into something more tangible. Here is what this process may sound like:

> SALESPERSON: "What we need to do now, Mr. Client, is pick a tentative Start Date for this project."
>
> CLIENT: "Well, I'm not sure I'm ready to do that yet. I don't even know if we're going to use your service or not."
>
> SALESPERSON: "That's fine. But for our own internal planning process, I need to pick a potential start date. I'm going to say . . . June 1."

Even though you came up with this date on your own, the more you use this date to launch your Mini-Step Planning process, the more that fact will become blurred and forgotten.

HOW TO DISPLAY THESE STEPS AND START DATE

There are no real rules for the best way to display the Mini-Steps to your clients. Some companies I've worked with simply have them listed on a single sheet of paper, while others choose to create elaborate and colorful printed documents. Some show nothing to clients at all, opting to do everything verbally. Again there are no rules, it's whatever works best for your particular situation.

A rule of thumb would probably be that the more elaborate and lengthy your sales process, the more elaborate your Mini-Step support documents should be. If you've got several levels of decision makers, budget processes, and proposal development stages, then you'll probably want to develop a fairly extensive, professionally prepared Mini-Step process to show clients. Conversely, if your sales cycle is very short, with few steps, there's probably no need to show the client anything.

I also suggest creating materials for your own use that will help keep the Mini-Steps fresh in your mind when you're in sales situations. You want to be able to see them when talking with clients, either on the phone or face-to-face. As you're closing for action, you want to keep closing for more action without having to go back to the office or having to make a return call. In the heat of the battle our minds have a tendency to freeze, and we may not be able to think of the next several steps. Produce the steps in an easy to read document that you can post on the wall of your cubicle or office, or condense them onto a card you can carry with you for easy access when making a call. Having them in writing also helps solidify the concept that "this is how we always do things—nothing unusual I'm asking for."

DEVELOPING A CLOSING PLAN

Once you've laid out the Mini-Steps and established a Closing Date, you can develop what I call a "Closing Plan," which is a strategic plan for bringing the client through the sales pipeline.

I hope you can see the difference between a Closing Plan that includes Mini-Steps and the old two-step model. Here is an example from a pro-football luxury suite salesperson:

A Closing Plan Using Mini-Steps

- Today's date: March 8

- Meet with client's sales and marketing team: March 23

- Stadium walk-through: April 1

- Participate in draft party: April 15

- Planned closing date: July 10

- First pre-season game: August 18

A Closing Plan Using the Normal Two-Step Process

- Today's date: March 8

- First pre-season game: August 18

Which closing plan is more consultative in nature?

Which one is actually more beneficial for the client?

Which one will give the seller and manager a better read on where truly is in the pipeline?

ASSIGNING A PERCENTAGE TO THE MINI-STEPS

Another strategic advantage of developing concrete Mini-Steps in the process is the ability to attach a percentage, or chance, that you'll close for a YES on each step in the process. So instead of having to guess based on a gut feel of the salesperson (more verbal interpretation), a manager is able to look at each step and assign a percentage based on the action step taken.

I get into this in much greater detail in Chapter 7, Consultative Closing for Managers, but basically the Mini-Steps enable the client to demonstrate, through action or in-action, where they are in the decision-making process, rather than a salesperson giving the manager an educated guess based on a "gut feeling."

This makes a huge difference in management accountability, planning, and the ability of the manager to hop in and help the salesperson.

Case Study on Developing Mini-Steps: Point B

Point B is a professional services firm focused exclusively on project leadership and execution. They work with organizations ranging from start-ups to Fortune 100 corporations, solving critical business problems. The firm was founded in 1995, and now has consultants based in Seattle (where the firm was started), Portland, Denver, Phoenix, and San Francisco.

I've been consulting with Point B since about 2003, primarily focusing on improving their business development (sales) process. The challenge Point B has in this area is they don't believe in hiring salespeople. Instead, they prefer to grow their business organically through doing great work, building strong relationships, and gaining client referrals—a process that is driven primarily by the Point B consultants. And while their consultants are certainly brilliant project managers and leaders, most of them are not experienced salespeople.

In fact, they are totally turned off to the "hard sell" closing strategies and negative characteristics normally associated with being in sales. (Who can blame them? These things turn most of us off, especially clients.)

So my challenge was to get these Point B consultants comfortable enough with the selling process to have success, without changing their personality or appearing too "salesy."

I started with Point B as I always do when consulting an organization, by looking at the sales process and the development of Mini-Steps. Ironically, Point B is a company that is engaged by some of the top companies in the world to help them do this exact process: break down complex problems into something more manageable, which involves the development of smaller, actionable steps. And even though this is what they do everyday for others, they had not applied the concept to their own sales process.

Jon Fleming, a managing director at Point B, is an experienced and gifted project manager and leader, who leads the firm's new business efforts. I asked Jon to explain how Point B tackles project management.

"When we're brought in to lead projects. Many times clients already have a plan in place, but they just can't seem to get the needed traction to move the project forward at an acceptable pace. The project may be stalled, making little or no progress. Frequently there is a common issue: They don't break things down into manageable-sized chunks. For example, maybe they are launching a new product, and one of the tasks on the project plan says *complete product design.* Well what does that mean? And the rule of thumb that we use is that if a task takes longer than 40 hours, then it's too big and needs to be broken down into smaller tasks. When you break a big task down into manageable chunks everyone can see that something is happening every week. We're moving the ball down the field—sometimes it's 10 yards, sometimes it's 20 or 30 yards—but we're moving toward the end goal. It's just like building a house: You have to get the plumbing done, the electrical installed, the house framed, and the foundation put in—there are four major tasks right there.

"Well, you can't manage to those tasks as they are, you need to break them down. Take the foundation and break it into bite-sized chunks: The first week we're going to survey the property, the 2nd week we're going to clear the trees, the 3rd week we're going to dig the ditch for the foundation, the 4th week we're going to put up the frames—that way you have specific manageable things you can track over a several week period. When you don't have these smaller steps to watch, it's much harder to see when you're getting off track until it's too late."

I joke with Jon all the time about how Point B has taken the whole concept of Mini-Step development to a stratospheric level, because where most clients I work with may have 10 to 12 steps in their process, Point B had about 35 (which he's trimmed down to around 28). And each step has an associated percentage of close attached to it! (See Table 3-1, Point B Mini-Steps and Associated Probability of Close.)

According to Jon, "A couple of things have happened with the implementation of Mini-Steps. First of all, they give me a lot better insight into what's really happening in the sales pipeline. Instead of just guess-

Table 3-1. The Point B Mini-Steps and Associated Probability of Close.

Point B Mini-Step	Close Probability
❏ Initial face to face meeting.	10%
❏ Develop and send a follow-up email to the prospect after the initial meeting.	10%
❏ Point B understands the prospects decision making process.	24%
❏ Client NDA signed.	26%
❏ Point B understands the prospect's background, organization, issues, and how we can help.	32%
❏ The prospect is willing to schedule a follow-up meeting to further discuss.	34%
❏ Identify and meet key stakeholders and/or executives in the organization (if they are required in the buying process).	42%
❏ Business problem and/or need identified.	46%
❏ Point B receives project background information.	48%
❏ Introduction to relevant project resources and key executives.	50%
❏ Client MSA in place.	54%
❏ Point B provides the prospect with references.	75%

❑ The prospect would like to interview Point B resources for an identified opportunity.	76%
❑ Point B staffing is secured.	90%
❑ SOW is drafted and reviewed.	95%
❑ Prospect signs the SOW.	100%

ing, or trying to figure out what an associate may say, I can track the process much more accurately. Before we had those Mini-Steps in place, an associate might meet with a client and have the following result: They'd have a decent conversation and come out of the meeting thinking 'that went pretty well.' Subsequently, I would guess what that meant and come up with a thought of my own, and meanwhile the client is thinking something completely different. So we had three people thinking completely different things about the exact same meeting.

"Another important aspect is that Mini-Steps have given the associates more step-by-step action to take in the process, so that they not only have a roadmap to follow, but they can see the progress that they're making along that map, or maybe are *not* making. And while they have all the steps listed, they know that not every step has to happen every time. But generally, these steps comprise the typical sequence of events that have to happen in order for me to get from an introductory meeting with a client to closing the sale.

"Look, our associates aren't salespeople, and they're not used to the way clients can act, or how they'll say something just to be nice, because most people like to be nice and not hurt your feelings. So they'd come out of these meetings feeling really good because the client said they may be *very interested in maybe doing something,* but with your Mini-Step process, folks can see that if the client fails to take action, no matter what they may have said, then it's probably not going to go anywhere. This is a major revelation for people who are not used to being in sales, and when they can see where clients are in the process, it really helps. Having the Mini-Steps in place gives me empirical data to reference, to be able to say, 'Listen, I know you had a great conversation, but if the client isn't ready to take step 22, they're not as far along as you thought.' This is also good for the client, because we can better recognize that there's an issue, and either we find out what it is and complete the sale, or determine, 'okay they're not ready to move forward right now, let's move on.' That way we can invest our resources elsewhere without taking up any more of their time.

"Lastly, Mini-Steps provide a very tangible way for associates to see their progress in the sales process. Historically, they may have become frustrated with the amount of time required to close a sale, and the lack of perceived progress when focusing only on the end goal. But, now they can see that it's more about moving the ball down the field a little at a time, constantly making progress.

"The Mini-Steps have also improved planning and sales forecasting, which is an important area for us because of the staffing component. If I have a perfect associate for a client project role, but then the sale doesn't go through, it has the potential of impacting our bottom line. With the Mini-Step process in place, I can

> get a much more accurate view of what is real and what is probably not so real in the pipeline, and then plan staffing accordingly."

FREQUENTLY ASKED QUESTIONS

Here are some frequently asked questions (FAQs) I get when developing Mini-Steps:

Q: *Isn't having a bunch of steps going to over-complicate and slow down the closing process?*

A: This is one of the first questions I get when outlining the Mini-Step process, and the concern makes sense. Sales processes are complicated enough, so why would we want to add ten more little steps? Two things to keep in mind: One, chances are you're doing some of these steps anyway; you just haven't thought about them and put them down on paper, or used them as tools to properly move the client toward closure. So, in reality you're not *adding* that many additional steps. And two, many of these steps can be done almost simultaneously, you don't have to do a step a day, or spread them out over weeks and months; they can all happen within minutes if need be. The reality is that the more you break down a project into smaller, bite-sized chunks, and then use those smaller chunks to gain continual buy-in and commitment, the faster and more efficient you become. You also increase your chances for executing with excellence.

Q: *Do you share all the Mini-Steps with clients during the process?*

A: It's totally up to you and the nature of your sales process. If you have the type of product or service that is very complicated and involved, with multiple decision makers and lots of different elements, then you may want to share more of the stages since you're getting buy-off from so many different people and different departments. If, however, you have a fairly simple and short sales cycle, then you may only need to have one or two action-oriented Mini-Steps that you share with clients. Typically, I encourage my clients to list all the Mini-Steps in the process, then highlight the ones you feel would be beneficial in educating, enlightening, or closing clients within the process.

Q: *Should you make the client sign off on the time-line and then give them a copy?*

A: I've helped clients develop Mini-Step project forms where there are places to write in tasks, assignments, and dates. Some have created them on duplicate paper so a copy can stay with a client and one with the salesperson. Others write down the information in front of the client then send over a printed time-line. It just depends on what works best given your client interaction and how important it is to be clear on the dates and deliverables. I think having some sort of document helps keep the project on course, and it also may help in keeping the roaming competitors at bay.

Q: *How often should you review your Mini-Steps?*

A: I would say on at least a quarterly basis. The things I would pay attention to are:

- Are there steps we don't need, or aren't using enough?

- Are there gaps where we could use an extra step?

- Are there more exciting, customer-centric steps we need to add to add value, as well as lock down the client earlier?

- Do we need to adjust the percentage of close associated with a particular Mini-Step?

REVIEW

• The Mini-Step Closing process is designed to be good not only for the salesperson, but for the client as well.

• Clients don't realize how stupid they can make clients feel in the questioning process.

• Consultative closing is designed to make the client feel smarter and more in control.

• There are several different types of Mini-Steps:
  —To-do Mini-Steps
  —Mini-Steps that help clients make good decisions
  —Mini-Steps to secure inventory, production, or delivery
  —Mini-Steps to help fulfill the order
  —Mini-Step special events for clients

• To help forecast opportunities in the pipeline, a percentage of a successful close can be attached to several of the Mini-Steps, such as "Get security clearance at client site—50 percent chance of a YES."

• There should be a "Start Date" established with every potential sale—basically a date in time from which we can plan backwards.

Bonus Materials Available at the Online Resource Center:

• More Mini-Step processes from real clients (great for using as a template for the development of your Mini-Step Plan)

CHAPTER 4

How to Use Mini-Steps
to Close for Action

I make people better Consultative Closers almost every day of my life, and there is nothing that gives me more satisfaction. Just knowing that I've helped someone who absolutely MUST become better at selling and closing or they won't survive, gives me a sense of satisfaction that no amount of money could buy. And I would like to do more of that exact thing in this chapter, where I'm going to show you *how* to use the Mini-Steps you've just created (or will soon create) to get clients to take action, and present more simple strategies for making major improvements in "your game."

And action is what it's all about.

I'm not sure how this whole verbal-only thing came about in sales. I mean, we've always had contracts and brochures and various other paperwork involved in the sales and implementation process, but for some reason we've relied almost exclusively on the salesperson and the client making verbal agreements to either move forward or not. And as we've discussed, because of the roles we play and the potential conflict of a sales call, there can be quite a bit of deception involved in the verbal back and forth, with words having multiple meanings and everything being clouded by the underlying agendas: clients wanting to avoid conflict and get rid of salespeople, and sellers desperately needing to hear positive things (even if they're not real).

So we're all about action, and the more Mini-Steps we have in the process, the more opportunities we have to get the client to either take action, or not take action, which is what we will use to determine how a client is actually "doing" in our sales pipeline.

I often use the analogy of a medical doctor when describing various elements within sales and the sales process. Action versus verbal is like the difference between the doctor using diagnostic tools and tests (e.g., EKGs, blood tests, X-rays) to determine how a patient is doing, versus making that diagnosis based solely on how a patient feels. ("How are you feeling?" "I'm feeling okay.") Can you imagine how many patients would die if doctors' treatments were based exclusively on how patients felt? Unfortunately, sales opportunities also die, or at least become stalled, when based on a salesperson's verbal assessment of "how things are going." Action steps allow the salesperson (and the doctor) to see how the client (the patient) is truly doing, in conjunction with how they say they feel.

Once we've identified our Mini-Steps, and concluded that they're to be used to get the client to take action, we still need to know:

- How to ask the right questions to get action

- How to effectively listen and probe

- How to respond to any number of answers we may get

For doctors it's not enough to just be able to diagnose a symptom, know all the medicines, and understand all the tools and equipment. They must also know how to question, how to listen, how to form relationships and gain trust, how to handle patient fear and anxiety, how to laugh and sometimes cry, and generally how to help patients make decisions and take action steps that may be outside the patients' comfort zones.

Sounds like a great model for a Consultative Closing salesperson, doesn't it?

FIRST WE MUST LEARN HOW TO ASK GOOD CLOSING QUESTIONS

Traditionally this is where consultative salespeople have always struggled: knowing how to ask to ask the tough closing questions without coming off as too pushy, or "salesy." I think much of this struggle has been a by-product of a flawed, or completely lacking, sales process, and the fact that everything was happening verbally between a nervous salesperson and a potentially deceptive client—both desperately trying to avoid conflict. Plus, without Mini-Steps defined in the process, there is nothing really to ask good questions about!

So sellers would trudge along, working in the empty spaces in between steps 1 and 2 in the old two-step process. After step 1, they only had one other step, the BIG step (the *you're sold* step) to talk about. So, the old-school closing questions were usually big and vague:

"Are we ready to get going on this today?"

"What's stopping us from saying YES to this right now?"

While these questions are okay and may still work in some situations, the big question here is, what is the meaning of the word *"this?"* In a typical two-step process, "THIS" normally meant the whole enchilada, the deal is done, *are you ready to buy?*

But it's just too big and too vague for most people (clients and sellers) to handle. Thus, it causes a good deal of potential conflict, which inevitably leads to the use of deception.

Now, thanks to our Mini-Step process, we have identifiable, smaller, action-oriented chunks we can ask about. This really changes the nature of the questions and the way they're asked. Instead of one loaded question about taking some vague action on one big thing, we're going to ask for more specific action to be taken on several smaller things.

It's amazing how a little thing like having an identifiable action step can improve a question. Let's use the previous examples and change them from asking about the one big sale to a specific action step:

> "Are you ready to get the *creative brainstorming meeting* on the books today?" (versus "Are we ready to get going on *this* today?")

> "What's stopping us from saying YES to at least *the tentative locations* today?" (versus "What's stopping us from saying YES to *this* right now?")

Notice the difference?

Another one of those wonderful byproducts of Mini-Step Closing is how much softer and less-pushy the salesperson's questions sound when zeroing in on one action step at a time. It's just easier for the client to say yes or no to a smaller thing than it is to some big, unclear, scary thing, as in *"Are we ready to get going on THIS?"* Again, this whole process is designed to be easier, and more enjoyable for the client, not just for us. *And this thought should always be at the heart of the Consultative Closer.*

You'll find that by asking about specific, smaller items, your questioning will be more forceful, but won't appear or feel that way to you, or to the client. Imagine being more forceful and direct, *and clients liking you more!* That is a definite win-win any way you look at it.

FOCUS ON THE STRUCTURE OF CONSULTATIVE CLOSING QUESTIONS

In addition to including a Mini-Step in your question, there are a few other simple steps you can take to improve the consultative closing questions you ask clients.

First let's review the *tone* of your questioning. As I just mentioned, you can be more forceful and direct when you've got a specific action step, and you can also be more *assumptive.* This comes from focusing not on the big thing, but on small, seemingly risk-free action steps that lend themselves to an assumptive tone.

We'll get into the actual wording in a moment, but generally an assumptive question starts with, "I'm assuming . . ." or "I would imagine . . ." or "I'm guessing. . . ." When you follow that with a small step, it's much easier to accept, and shouldn't panic the buyer. It's breaking down the big, possibly scary thing into the small, "nothing to fear" steps.

Imagine you're a frightened flyer, scared to death of leaving the ground in a giant metal tube. (Gee, what's there be afraid of?) If the flight attendant simply came on the overhead speaker and asked, "Well, are we ready to do THIS?" it might freak you out. *Whoa there cowboy, what is this THIS you're talking about?*

Instead, they have a wonderful "Mini-Step Process," or check-list, they run through, all done with a smile (sometimes), and a pleasing, assuring, and comforting voice.

"Please just buckle your seatbelts low and tight across your lap." (You think, *Hey, I can do that, do it all the time, no problem. Click!*)

"Turn off all electronic devices." (*Sure, why not? Love to turn this phone off.*)

"An oxygen mask will. . . ." (*Now wait a minute. . . .*)

You get the point: When you've got small, safe, action steps it's much easier to be assumptive in what you say to clients. In fact, what's actually happening is that we're moving away from *questioning* and into actually *suggesting* with what I call an Assumptive Suggestion.

An Assumptive Suggestion

As you're working with a client, showing her the various Mini-Steps you have in your process, you'll *need* to get action (either YES or NO). You'll have a much better chance at getting action if you simply make an *Assumptive Suggestion* versus just an *ask*. Here is an example of an Assumptive Suggestion:

"At this point, with six months to go before the official launch date of your accounting system, I would strongly suggest we at least get a meeting set up with your HR people and our training team to plan a possible implementation and orientation training schedule. When should we schedule that?"

Let's break down this Assumptive Suggestion to look at the critical ingredients that I recommend you include in your closing process:

1. *"At this point"*
This is acknowledging that, while the actual sale or buying of the product or service is going to take place at some point in the future (a seemingly safe distance), there are tasks to be accomplished right now, *at this point.* Other words and phrases that mean the same thing are:
"This early on . . . "
"At this stage . . . "
"Though we've got time . . . "

2. *"Strongly suggest"*
This is an interesting phrase because of the mixture of the words: *strongly*—a bold and urgent plea, and *suggest*—a softer word that means the salesperson may be right, but it's only an opinion, and the buyer still may override the seller. Other words and phrases that mean the same thing are:
"Highly recommend . . . "
"Strongly urge . . . "

3. *"At least"*
This phrase is probably the one I use most when I'm doing Mini-Step Closing, because it speaks to the nature of Mini-Steps themselves. *It's not the WHOLE sale right here, right now, it's just a small step,* and we can *at least* take action on THAT, right, Ms. Client? This is also effective because it appeals to the deeper need of the client to fix their problem (and they know down deep they need to fix their problem), though it still acknowledges their outer nature to procrastinate and take it slow.

I think of when I was out buying some new suits and sport coats. I have a tendency to procrastinate in this area for several reasons, mainly because I don't trust my own judgment when it comes to figuring out what's in style, or what matches. If a salesperson senses this, and has a Mini-Step process in mind, she could say: "Well I know you're a bit nervous about this, Greg, so let's AT LEAST get your measurements in the computer and I'll pull together some shirt and tie combinations that could work with your skin tone. AT LEAST you'll have that in moving forward." Now that makes sense, because she's acknowledging my instinct to procrastinate and move slowly, while I'm satisfying my inner need to fix my problem and get me some nicer clothes. Other words and phrases that mean the same thing are:

"If nothing else . . ."

"At this stage . . . "

4. *"Possible"*

This is what I call a "pressure release" word. It is used right before an action-step to soften it, and it allows the client to feel he is still in control of the outcome. What makes it powerful is that while it suggests that there may NOT be an implementation, there also MAY be one. It enables the client to visualize this in the future, creating a powerful ownership image that is part of the transfer of ownership involved in sales. Other words and phrases that mean the same thing are:

"Tentative . . . "

"Potential . . . "

"Feasible . . . "

5. *"When should we schedule that?"*

We MUST remember to ask the client to take action. Just because our steps are simple and fairly risk-free, we still need to make that ask. Other words and phrases that mean the same thing are:

"What day works best for you?"

"Let's get started, shall we?"

Exercise

You can take this templated outline to create your own Assumptive Suggestions. Just fill in the blanks using the words or phrases I've suggested, then add your specific action steps.

"At this point *(insert the phrase you want or use this one)* _____,
with six months *(insert your time frame)* _____
to go before the official launch date of your accounting system, *(insert your sale information)*

_____

I would strongly suggest *(insert the phrase you want)* _____
we at least *(insert the phrase you want or use this one)* _____
get a meeting set up with your HR people and our training team to plan a possible implementation and orientation training *schedule (insert your own Mini-Step)* _____
When should we schedule that?" *(insert your own "Ask for the action")* _____

Modifying Normal Questions into More Action-Oriented Questions

In addition to the Assumptive Suggestion, we can take normal sales questions and turn them into more action-oriented questions that require an answer. Here are a few examples:

Normal Sales Question:
"Does this look like something you'd like to do?"

Action-Oriented Question:
"Is this (insert action step) something you'd like to do?" (I removed "Does" and "look like" to improve the question.)

Normal Sales Question:
"So, what do you say? Are you ready to go?"

Action-Oriented Question:
"So, are we ready to at least go with the (insert action step)?"

Normal Sales Question:
"Can you see a reason why we can't move forward?"

Action-Oriented Question:
"Can you see a reason why we can't move on (insert action step)?"

As you can see, you don't have to do a total questioning make-over. You simply add action steps and you're going to start getting clearer answers.

However, you need to watch what you wish for, because when you ask more action-oriented, clear questions, you're not going to get back as many vague platitudes, or wishy-washy neutral-zone answers (e.g., "We're interested"). Instead, you're going to get a reply, and that reply is going to be a combination of their verbal answer and—more important—their physical response: Either they're going to do it, or they're not, which will give you clear direction forward or backward, and you need to learn how to deal with either answer.

HOW TO EFFECTIVELY *LISTEN* AND OBSERVE THE RESPONSE—THEN RESPOND

With Consultative Closing we not only need to learn how to ask more action-oriented questions, we must also learn how to move beyond the verbal response of the client (who may be saying something falsely positive), and focus on observing their action or nonaction. Once we've observed it, we must accept the result and respond accordingly.

Over my years in sales and sales training, I've seen many workshops, books, and research materials that are focused on improving listening skills. And it's an important topic because sellers by and large *are* terrible listeners. But I think maybe we've missed the boat a bit here. For while the act of listening is important, perhaps what's more important is the study of action or nonaction on the part of the client; even the best of listeners are still operating on a verbal-only level.

So I'm going to redefine "listening" as not only *hearing* the verbal response, but also *watching* the physical response around an action step. Chances are, we'll see there are many incongruities between what is being said and what is actually being done. For instance, a client may *say,* "We're fairly interested," but then will refuse to take even the smallest of action steps. If they're as interested as they say, then they would take an action step, right? If not, something is wrong, something is out of whack. There are hidden issues, and we can then get at the issues. Now I can only pick that up if I'm fully "listening" as we've defined it (listening and watching).

Words are fine, and we should learn how to listen to them and pick them apart. But they're only words; without action, they mean nothing. Action or nonaction are the only things we should truly value in the sales process.

The question then becomes, are salespeople, who we've already established can be codependent in the deceptive sales interaction, willing and able to *accept what they observe (verbally and physically) and react accordingly?* What I mean is, if the client is asked a direct action-oriented question, and she *doesn't* take action, will the salesperson accept and acknowledge this for what it represents, or just pretend it didn't happen and proceed as if everything is okay? And if the client *does* take action, will the salesperson recognize this for what *it* is, and be bold enough to get the client to take another action step on the way to the close?

There are only two possible responses (which are more than "answers") to a Mini-Step question:

YES or NO
NOTHING ELSE EXISTS

Yes or No. Consultative salespeople have been taught to avoid questions that could end in one of these two answers. Those, we were told over and over, are "close-ended" questions, and salespeople were usually afraid of getting a quick NO. Besides, we should be focused on "open-ended" questions, questions that force clients to explain and talk more.

Yes or No was to be avoided, and here I come along

saying that what we're *after* is YES or NO, and that in fact, *they're the only answers that exist!* Some explanation is no doubt in order.

First of all, I agree wholeheartedly with using open-ended rather than close-ended questions when we're interviewing and talking with clients. Anything that gets the client to open up and tell us how they feel beneath the surface of a one-word answer is good. However, what we're talking about here is just . . . *talking.* It's the exchange of verbal questions and answers between client and seller. And what I'm talking about with the focus on YES or NO is all about an outcome: An action is either taken, or not taken.

We need to really, really get this point, because it's at the heart of Consultative Closing: There are only two possible *responses* to an action request *for today:* YES, let's take action today, or NO, let's not take action today. Everything else in between that we may verbally discuss (e.g., all future promises to possibly take action) really mean nothing, at least as far as today is concerned. Either the client takes action or he doesn't.

There is no gray area.

There is no "fence" to sit on.

Now, this doesn't mean the client won't take action tomorrow. It only means that for today, there was no action, which means it was a NO FOR TODAY.

Let's talk about MAYBE. I'm not suggesting that there aren't people who start at MAYBE and then go to YES. In fact I'm sure there are many of them. But it still doesn't change the fact that MAYBE is still NO FOR TODAY, right? Yes, the client MAY be a YES tomorrow, but for right now, for today, it's a NO.

Let me demonstrate further with an analogy from my

house, which involves getting my teenage daughters to do their chores. For instance, one of the chores is to take their clean clothes up from the laundry and to their room.

I will walk into the family room where my little cherubs are watching TV, and before looking in the laundry room, I like to ask a direct question, "Did you take your clothes up to your room?" Now there are only two possible responses: "Yes, I did," or "No, I did not." "Maybe I did" doesn't really work as an answer, because whatever they say will be backed up by the evidence, either I'm going to open that laundry room door and see the basket, telling me the clothes did NOT go to her room, or I'm going to look and see the basket is gone, telling me the clothes DID go to their room. There is no such thing as *maybe* seeing the basket. It's a simple question, with a simple answer, right? Not with teenagers.

Here are the variety of answers my daughters can give when I ask, "Did you take your clothes up to your room? Yes or No?"

"YES, I am going to, Dad." (Sounds fine, but still equals NO.)

"YES, I WILL." (Sounds firm, but still equals NO.)

"Of course, I 'get it' . . . and I plan on doing it." (Sounds industrious, but it's still NO.)

This means I must clarify what I've heard and help usher in a little concept we call *reality:* "I appreciate all that, but let's clarify. The answer is really, 'NO, we didn't take our clothes up to our room.' Right?"

The same holds true for clients. When asked to take action, they'll sometimes try to pretend there is another world in between YES and NO. Like teenagers, they like to throw out a possible positive outcome to keep the salesperson (parent) at bay.

When asked, clients may respond with answers like:

Action Oriented Question:
    "So, are we ready to at least go with setting up the website?" (Our action step.)

Client (Teenager) Answers:
    "YES, I am going to do that eventually . . ." equals "NO" (for today).

    "I AM ABSOLUTELY going to look into that . . ." equals "NO."

    "I CERTAINLY WOULD like to do something like that soon . . ." equals "NO."

We will talk about how to "embrace NO" in Chapter 5, but for now we just need to learn to clarify the position for what it is, just like I did with my daughters' clothes.

Because we're equipped to deal with reality—and in reality there can be only two possible outcomes to an action-oriented question—we have to clarify the situation in order to move on.

WAYS TO CLARIFY MAYBE

When the client responds with a wishy-washy answer about a possible YES answer in the future, I usually start by asking, "But not today, right?"

CLIENT: "Well, yes, I think we'll eventually have to do that."

ME: "I see. But it doesn't sound like you're ready to do that today?"

CLIENT: "No, you're right. I'm not."

Then we have to clarify that we've arrived at one of our two reality check-points: YES or NO.

> **ME:** "So really, for the sake of clarity (softener), we're at a NO, at least for now (softener), right?"

> **CLIENT:** "Yes, that's right."

Clients just aren't used to this level of reality, and certainly aren't used to going to "the NO place." And they may actually fight you on it.

> **CLIENT:** "Well, I wouldn't say I'm at a NO . . ."

> **ME:** "Oh really, so are you saying you may be ready today?"

Before we move ahead to dealing with either the YES or the NO outcome, we have to clearly identify reality.

Outcome 1: YES

What to Do if We Get a YES Answer to a Mini-Step Closing Question

> **SALESPERSON:** "At this point, with six months to go before the official launch date of your accounting system, I would strongly suggest we at least get a meeting set up with your HR people and our training team to plan a possible implementation and orientation training schedule. When do we want to schedule that?"

> **CLIENT:** "Well, how about next Wednesday at 10?"

Once a client agrees to an action step, the salesperson must seize the moment and be specific with her actions. If in this situation she were to respond with, "Okay, good. I'll get back with you and let you know when we can do that," she may end up in the exact same place, but this time she's giving the verbal approval.

I've found that salespeople, especially consultative-oriented salespeople, can be so anxious to get away from the pressures and potential conflict of the sales call, they'll exit various sales situations way too early, even situations where the client has expressed a positive response, or a desire to move forward! The salesperson, sensing this crazy need to split, will say, "Let me give you a call next week and we can get this going," or "Let me go back to the office and put some things together and give you a call."

Why are they leaving? Why aren't they taking as many concrete action steps as possible when they've got a live, breathing, positive client sitting right there? It seems like a ridiculous thing to do, but many people are so attached to being liked, they just want to get the heck out of the situation now.

I remember doing a ride-along with a salesperson a few years ago as part of a consulting and coaching engagement with an East Coast television station. The young advertising salesperson I was with had been selling for about two years, and was moderately successful. He had a fun personality and people liked him, but his managers were concerned because he was struggling with closing deals.

During our sales call with the top manager of a small chain of high-end men's clothing stores, the problems this seller was having became very clear to me when he moved into the final stages of the call, when it was time for the client to take action. The client was ready to move forward, and the salesperson was suggesting steps that required a delay!

Here is how this conversation sounded:

CLIENT: "I think it makes sense for us to do something with your station . . ."

SALESPERSON: "Great. Why don't I work some things up and get back with you on setting a time for your ad production?"

CLIENT: "Sounds good." (Clients aren't going to do the seller's job and ask, "Should we take an action step now?")

SALESPERSON: "Okay, are you going to be in tomorrow? I'll call you once I know about studio time."

CLIENT: "I'm not in tomorrow. Call me early next week and I'll see about setting something up." (By next week we may be dealing with a whole different mindset, or someone from another station could have poisoned the well.)

I just couldn't help myself, I had to step in and take over the call (and I HATE to do that on ride-along meetings).

ME: "You know I was just thinking about this. We NEED to schedule that studio time right now, just to make sure we can get in . . . because we also need to schedule the right talent and they can get very busy. Mr. Client, can you do a Thursday or Friday afternoon? Those are times when we can usually get in?"

CLIENT: "I think so. Let me get my calendar."

I wasn't making up the fact that pre-booking studio time was the best way to ensure space and the right talent, though we still might have been able to book it in a week.

But why take the risk? And why not use this step to lock down the client at the same time?

The salesperson did a great job in getting the client ready to accept a solution to his challenges—he was ready to sign on to any plan the salesperson put forward—but the seller's plan was to go back to the station and call back. So, of course, the client instinctively loves that plan: "You mean I don't have to commit? Great!"

When we got back in the car I asked him why he wanted to leave and then call later for steps he could have knocked down right there, on the spot?

"Well, he seemed ready to go, I just didn't want to push him too hard," he explained.

"You're right, he was ready to go, you did a great job of discovering needs and making a solid presentation. But what do you mean by 'pushing him too hard'? How is penciling in studio time, something you're going to call about and do next week, pushing too hard? Isn't it actually better for the client if he books the time now versus next week?" I asked, trying to be as positive as possible.

"Well, yeah, I guess that makes sense, but I still think he's being straight with me," the seller said, still trying to justify his weak close.

"You're right, he may telling the truth. But when you ask you find out for sure, right?"

We have to learn to be more comfortable with the discomfort that is required when clients are trying to process things and make their decisions. Seizing the moment after a positive answer to a Mini-Step question means responding with an action step: "Okay, good. I've got our group's calendar right here. Let's pencil in something now. Does the last Friday of the month work for you?"

Once the client has taken action on a Mini-Step, the salesperson should review where that step is within the time-line and, if it makes sense, press for more action steps while the client is right there. If the salesperson has a full time-line printed out, he can just start attaching dates to tasks, working his way up to the point of close and perhaps beyond: "While we're at it, we need to go ahead and schedule a potential installation date so our equipment people can keep it in the order. . . ."

Simple Step: Need vs. Like

Substituting the word NEED for the word LIKE can have a dramatic impact on the urgency and sense of conviction on the part of the salesperson:

- I *need* to schedule an installation date . . .

- I'd *like* to schedule an installation date . . .

Need is NOW, like is LATER.
Need says MUST, like says SHOULD.
Need conveys URGENCY, like conveys WHENEVER IT'S CONVENIENT.

Steps for Handling a YES Answer to a Mini-Step

1. Seize the moment and be specific with your action step, including who is doing what and when.

2. If it makes sense, get the client to take as many additional action steps as possible, right then and there.

3. Don't be too quick to leave (so you can celebrate the victory). At the same time, don't "oversell" your way out of it. Just keep taking action step after action step.

Outcome 2: NO

What to Do If We Get a NO Answer to a Mini-Step Closing Question

> SALESPERSON: "At this point, with six months to go before the official launch date of your accounting system, I would strongly suggest we at least get a meeting set up with your HR people and our training team to plan a possible implementation and orientation training schedule. When do we want to schedule that?"
>
> CLIENT: "Well, I don't want to schedule that. . . ."

If a client doesn't agree to an action step, IT'S CRITICAL THAT THE SALESPERSON ACKNOWLEDGES THIS AND NOT PRETEND THAT IT DIDN'T JUST HAPPEN, such as: "Okay, well, I thought I'd try. I'll be back in touch later on and see where we are."

We will go into the shadowy, murky world of NO in Chapter 5 and learn how to embrace it as an answer. For now, I want to simply acknowledge that it exists and that when a client doesn't take action on a Mini-Step it's a signal that something may be wrong. *There may be issues,* and they need to be fully revealed and dealt with if there is any hope in moving the sale forward.

Those client issues *could* be:

- We haven't established enough value for the investment.

- A competitor has "poisoned the well."

- Someone inside the company has an allegiance to another company.

- The client doesn't like or trust us for whatever reason.

- The client hasn't accepted they have a problem or need.

The reality is, we just don't know. And we shouldn't be in the habit of guessing, or worse, pretending these issues don't exist, hoping they'll just go away over time.

Nothing in sales happens 100 percent of the time. Sometimes clients who don't have issues may still refuse to take action steps, and sometimes clients who have issues may take early action steps. But those percentages are small. Typically clients with issues won't take action, and those who don't have issues will take early action steps.

The key is to listen and observe with a critical ear, and when we get nonaction, we must learn how to accept it for what it is and not put on our rose-colored glasses and pretend nothing is wrong. If we don't get at the issues we can't address them and possibly move the sale forward.

It's also important to control our emotions and our body language when we get a NO. We can't have an attitude like, "GREAT, thanks for nothing!" and then slam our notebook closed. We have to accept it gracefully and learn how to ask a few follow up questions so we understand exactly what issues we may be dealing with. We will extend this post-negative response in more detail coming up in Chapter 5 on Embracing NO.

Here is an example of a salesperson asking the client to take action on a Mini-Step, then realizing there may be some issues leading to a NO.

SALESPERSON: "At this point, with six months to go before the official launch date of your accounting system, I would strongly suggest we at least

get a meeting set up with your HR people and
our training team to plan a possible implementation and orientation training schedule."

CLIENT: "Well, let's not do that quite yet."

SALESPERSON: (silence) "Okay, sounds like you're not
comfortable taking this step, Mr. Client. What
are your concerns at this point?"

Remember, clients can have a hard time telling us bad
news, and it will take some coaxing to get at the truth:

CLIENT: "Well, I'm not sure I have *concerns*. I'm just
early in the process, and still looking at a few
other folks. . . ."

Because of the client's desire to avoid conflict through
using deception, I have a tendency to be skeptical about
what clients say when they won't take action. I have to keep
digging at the truth, even when the truth is ugly:

SALESPERSON: "I understand what you're saying. But
let's take other people out of the equation for a
moment. I sense there are still issues with our
product. You're not 100 percent on board with
our solution at this point, are you?"

Here are some initial steps when getting a NO response. We will cover the NO response in much greater
detail coming up in Chapter 5 on "Embracing NO."

Steps for Handling a NO Answer to a Mini-Step

1. Accept the answer for what it is. It is a NO-FOR-
NOW, it's not a MAYBE.

2. Don't be defensive. Don't attack. Change your body language (e.g., lean back). Relax.

3. Assume the client has issues or concerns, and ask them to share those concerns.

The faster you can really grasp the reality that there are only two possible outcomes for a question on taking action TODAY—either YES or NO—and that everything that is not YES is a NO-FOR-NOW, the better off you'll be. Just burn these thoughts into your head and act accordingly:

Maybe = NO-FOR-NOW

Interested = NO-FOR-NOW

Call me tomorrow = NO-FOR-NOW

What we'll discover in Chapter 5 is that NO-FOR-NOW is a far, far better answer than anything neutral.

CLOSING ON REMOVED DECISION MAKERS USING MINI-STEPS

One of the best uses of Mini-Steps within the closing process is in dealing with removed decision makers (RDMs) and lower level decision makers (LLDMs). These are the various people involved in the client's decision making process: Some may be situated in the same office, while others could be in offices in different cities and even different countries. And although it's a wonderful goal to say, "I'm only going to deal with the top decision makers," you're still going to find yourselves in situations where you're dealing with multiple people with varying degrees of responsibility and decision-making power.

The first step to effectively dealing with RDMs and LLDMs (because you can never just wipe them out completely) is to fully expose the situation before you get too deep into the selling process. If you're doing an effective job in consultative selling, you will have gathered all the information about the client's decision-making process early on in the selling cycle. In my selling system I call this process "the Three Ps":

The Three Ps

People: Understanding who all the people are in the process

Path: Knowing the path the decision has to make

Power: Knowing how much power the person I'm in front of has

Chances are if we're selling just about anything these days, we're going to be dealing with lots of LLDMs and RDMs. Even on simple items sold to individuals, that person may have accountants to check with, or buddies, or family members. In order to be an effective Consultative Closer we need to know how to deal with these time-gobbling speed bumps.

Main Challenges We Have in Dealing with LLDMs and RDMs

•   The decision-making process is a wonderful escape area many clients like to use when feeling the heat and pressure of a hard-charging salesperson. Clients have no problem making up people, processes, budgets, issues—

whatever it takes to escape when that sales clock comes on. I find that the earlier you ask about the Three Ps the less likely you are to get deception, because the client isn't feeling any heat. And they *will* provide this information, but only if they're asked. They will usually not volunteer it up front.

•   It's typically tough to read just where your client ranks as far as being able to make a decision on YOUR product or service, because clients like to defuse this pressure (conflict avoidance) by bringing up other people. Assuming, for example, that your client is an LLDM:

> LLDM: "I'll listen to what you've got to say, but then you'll have to talk to Tom, Dick, and I believe Harry will want in on this as well. . . ."

•   It's often very difficult to gain access to the other LLDMs and RDMs, or to figure out what the other players value, what they like and dislike, and so forth.

•   Because we're flying so blind with the person we're selling, as well as with the next several levels within the decision-making process, we fall prey to delays, stalls, and general uncertainty as to exactly where the decision will finally be made.

WHAT WE MUST DO TO IMPROVE THE SITUATION

Although this book is not a full study on the earlier stages of the sales process, where we're dealing with the decision-making process, here are some quick tips I will share with you:

•   *The key is early knowledge.* Clients are more likely to lie and be deceptive later on in the sale cycle when we're trying to close. And here's a pet peeve of mine: When you ask about the decision-making process, PLEASE ASK:

> "Can you share with me the decision-making process?" Don't say: "Who besides yourself makes the decision?" which is not particularly flattering, sort of like saying, "There HAS to be someone else involved in this. I mean, look at you. Come on, who else is involved?"

• ***Understand what you can close on with the person you're with.*** Some LLDMs and RDMs make lots of decisions and go to the next level just for confirmation, while others make very few decisions and go to the next level for approval—you just don't know unless you ask. It's very dangerous to assume in this area.

• ***Make sure the person you're with is TRULY on board, and not just saying it to avoid pressure.*** This is a huge, huge area I find with salespeople, especially with consultative salespeople who tend to be a bit nicer; they just assume the LLDM or RDM they're dealing with is closed for a YES. This is an extremely dangerous assumption, because it's usually not true! LLDMs and RDMs will just pretend to be on board so they can blame the next level of decision maker and get the pressure off themselves.

Think about a job interview, where we're usually dealing with multiple decision makers in the process. Most people make the same mistakes I'm talking about here:

1. We don't find out about others in the process until very late in the game, *only because we don't ask.*

2. We don't know whether the person we're with can make any decisions, or what level of influence he may have, if any at all, *only because we don't ask.*

3. We don't know for sure if the person we're with is
   going to recommend us at the end of our interview,
   only because we don't ask.

I've found that clients are happy to give you all the
information you want, but you MUST ASK: They won't volunteer it.

MINI-STEPS TO THE RESCUE!

Mini-Steps are truly magical when you are dealing with
LLDMs and RDMs. While you can't wave a wand and
make a complicated decision-making process go away, you
can trim weeks and even months off your sales cycle.

How Mini-Steps are Used with LLDMs and RDMs

•   We will be using our identifiable action-steps to
get confirmation of true buy-in at various points in the sale.
And without buy-in, the sale isn't going to progress very far.
If LLDMs and RDMs aren't closed for a YES themselves,
they just won't show it to the next level, or if they do, they'll
put enough negative spin on it to poison any chance you
might have had. An action-step buy-in is much stronger
than the normal *verbal buy-in,* or worse, the *assumed buy-in*
most salespeople operate with:

> If an LLDM does not take action on a safe, risk-
> free Mini-Step, she is trying to communicate that
> either she doesn't buy into what you're selling, or
> she doesn't think she can sell it at the next level, so
> why bother.

•   Mini-Steps help gain momentum. When an LLDM
decides to take one or two action-steps, she may *need* the

momentum of these steps to help persuade the next person in the decision-making chain.

• Once the LLDM we're with decides to take an action-step, we can begin to look at the next level of decision makers in the process and determine what Mini-Step each person should be considering. I think a major mistake salespeople make is not spending enough time talking about the other people and other steps in the process with the one LLDM or RDM they're with, who I believe know much more than they let on about whether this next person will take an action-step or not. They'll also know the objections, stalls, and issues the others will have, but again, they aren't going to just volunteer it. You've got to ask.

HOW TO CLOSE LLDMS AND RDMS USING MINI-STEPS

Most salespeople (especially consultative salespeople because of our nature) struggle continuously with this one part of sales: closing LLDMs—getting them to take action on *something* and not just passing the decision down the line. Even experienced salespeople, who should know better and who've been through training, can fall back into bad habits and end up accepting nondecisions from LLDMs and RDMs.

It's easy to see why this happens, even to those of us who know what to expect—passing the decision on to others is done so easily and so often that it becomes second nature and acceptable to both parties. Clients like it because it ends the call without much conflict, and sellers like it because it gives them a good story back at the office and allows them to put another "warm prospect" in the sales pipeline, which can be a false security blanket.

Of all the sales problems and challenges I hear about from salespeople and sales managers, closing LLDMs and RDMs always comes up at or near the top of the list. The type of comments I usually hear are things like:

> "I can get one guy excited about it, but then it just dies."

> "There are always two or three people involved, and different budgets, plans, and priorities."

> "When I close one person, he can't even get me a meeting with the next level of the company. It just gets stuck there."

> "I honestly don't know if the person I'm dealing with can really make the decision or not."

We all struggle in this area. Clients are well trained in how to deal with salespeople, and they probably get more practice at it than we do. The hard part is really knowing how much of what you're hearing is real, and how much is a smoke screen designed to get rid of us.

Here are some simple steps that should help:

How to Deal with the LLDM

•   You must isolate. . . . isolate . . . isolate . . . the one you're with (assuming of course that you've determined this is the person you should be in front of to begin with). By *isolate* I mean you should ask them to *tune out* all other people and approval steps (such as budgets or funding) in the process:

> "Mr. Client, I know you've got several other folks involved in this decision-making process, including your silent partner (clients love to make up silent

partners). However, I'd like to focus just on you for today, and let's just assume these other people weren't involved at all, okay?"

• Clients may say "yeah, sure," but they'll often continue to bring up these other people. We need to keep asking them to focus just on where they are personally. I like to appeal to their ego a bit when this happens:

"You've mentioned your partners a few times now, and I can appreciate you're needing to speak with them. However, let's be honest. If you're not excited about this, and you're not buying into it, it's never going to go anywhere, am I right?"

• We need to know the Mini-Steps we can close on at each level of the process, with each decision maker. We have to have a plan because clients have no idea what's supposed to happen.

• We need to be clear with the LLDM we're with and ask for a decision (YES or NO) on a Mini-Step, rather than accept a verbal or assumed confirmation (which is all most other salespeople ever ask for). Here's an example of a typical verbal assumption. (I can't show you the *assumed confirmation* because . . . well, it's just *assumed.*)

SALESPERSON: "So, Mr. Client, you seem to like a lot of what I'm presenting here, right?"

CLIENT: "Yeah, I like a lot of it." (*There's also a lot I DON'T like, but the seller never seems to care about that.*)

SALESPERSON: "Okay, good. Let's talk about the next level in your process here."

• If salespeople even bother to ask LLDMs how they feel, they do it in this soft, vague, wishy-washy way.

We need to be more focused in the action steps we ask for and in listening to the answer.

• We're going to use the same Assumptive Suggestion type of close with the LLDM we're in front of, and we may add a phrase acknowledging others in the process, which is a preemptive strike to take this excuse away. The objective is to focus and close the one we're with:

> SALESPERSON: "Mr. Client, I know there are several others involved in the decision-making process, but if I could just focus on you at this point? We at least need to get the early fully-refundable deposit down on that corner suite. How did you want to take care of that?"

• If the client balks at taking this step, try a commitment step lower down in the process, one with less risk. If they continue to hedge and balk at moving forward, then something is wrong: Either they personally don't want your product or service, or they don't feel the next level will want it and they aren't comfortable selling it. You need to know those reasons.

Once You've Closed the LLDM

• If you get a personal NO from the LLDM, you need to handle it the same way you would a NO from the main decision maker: Mainly, you need to find out the reasons and discover what the world would look like in order for them to be at a YES. (We'll cover this in more detail, along with how to bring them back from NO, in Chapter 5.)

• If you get a personal YES from the LLDM, and you've tested this with an action-step, you'll want to *work with the decision maker* you've just closed to look at the other decision makers involved. (Again, this is assuming you've questioned extensively about the People, Path, and Power involved in the decision making process.)

> SALESPERSON: "Thanks for moving forward, at least as far as you personally can, Roger. Now let's focus for a moment on your partner. What is the first landmine we're going to be walking into with him?"

> Note: I like to go right to the negative thoughts the next decision maker could be feeling rather than ask, "What do you think he'll say," which will usually lead to a generic, neutral response such as, "He'll probably like a lot of it." When you go right to the negatives, you'll get at reality much faster.

• Once you've asked about the next-level decision maker and the potential landmines you're likely to walk into, you need to find out how effective your initial decision maker (the one you just closed) will be when presenting your product and addressing the concerns. You do this by asking, "How are you going to handle that when it comes?" and then listen closely to the response:

> CLIENT: "The biggest landmine with Bob? Well, it's probably going to be the cost. He's been concerned about spending over the past few months."

> SALESPERSON: "Okay, so when he says that to you, that he's concerned about the return on the investment in our product to solve your missing data problems, what will your response be?"

• Listen carefully to the response of the decision maker you're working with. If the response is quick, targeted, passionate, and to the point, it tells you two things: 1) Your initial decision maker truly "bought it" and gets it. 2) He will have a better shot at selling it at the next level (if you can't be there yourself, which you should still try to set up). Conversely, if the initial decision maker isn't very clear and quick with a response, it should tell you two entirely different things: 1) The issue he mentioned as a landmine for the next level is probably *his* issue. 2) He's going to have a hard time convincing anyone when he doesn't believe what he's saying.

•   If you get a less-than-enthusiastic response, you'll need to circle back and deal with it with your decision maker:

> SALESPERSON: "It sounds a little like you're not 100 percent convinced of the return on investment yourself. Is that accurate?"

•   Chances are you're going to have to create support materials to help the decision maker you're with to make the presentation to the partner. Here are a few ideas to try:

> You can try getting an invite to the meeting with the partner, or perhaps be conference-called in at the right time.

> You can set up a lunch meeting and invite everyone involved to come and hear the presentation.

> You can create some simple presentation pieces that can be delivered by your decision maker to the partner without a lot explanation.

•   Keep in mind that Mini-Steps that are taken by your decision maker can actually help build momentum to help sell other people in the chain. For example, if I'm a lower-level manager, and I'm trying to get a new accounting software in place but know I'm going to run into resistance from my bosses at corporate, I should be very receptive to any Mini-Steps I can get to help build momentum. It's sort of like when we were kids and we'd build momentum in the decision-making process by saying things like, "We already talked to Dan's dad, and he said he'd pick us up and pay for it," So as the lower level manager, I want to help build momentum by saying to my boss at corporate, "I at least got us signed up for a free demonstration and analysis they're doing next week," or "I got the guy to throw in four additional seats and free training for our upper management, but we have to install by March 31. I tentatively told him to pencil in the 27th and told him I'd try to push this through." I would only take one of these action-steps as a lower-level manager if I truly want the product, for why would I want to build momentum for something I don't want to see happen?

SOME FREQUENTLY ASKED QUESTIONS ABOUT HOW TO CLOSE USING MINI-STEPS

Q: *You say there are only two possible outcomes to an action-oriented question—YES or NO—but I know a lot of people who say MAYBE, and then go on to buy. Are you suggesting we should write them off because you say that MAYBE equals NO?*

A: No, I'm not saying that at all. I'm only focused on that moment in time. NO-FOR-NOW may be YES in twenty minutes. I've seen it happen many times. The thing we must realize is that MAYBE doesn't really exist as a physical outcome (it DOES exist as a verbal answer) to a direct question about an action-step. Suppose your defined action-step was to get a down payment check from the client. When you get back to the office and someone asks you, "Did you get the check or did you not?" it's not possible that MAYBE you have gotten it. You can say, "Maybe I did" until you're blue in the face, or until someone slaps you, but soon the truth will come out: Either you hand over a check or you don't. It's either YES I did, or NO I didn't.

Q: *If you get a YES answer to a Mini-Step question, how many steps should you keep on taking right there? Don't you run the risk of maybe getting a NO?*

A: I'd go for as many action-steps as make sense while you're in front of the client. And if I get a NO, or resistance, the earlier the better in my book. Either I can deal with it, or flush it out of the pipeline right there and now.

Q: *When dealing with lower level decision makers (LLDMs), how can you go around them if you're not getting anywhere, or they've said NO to you?*

A: All the more reason to call at the top and bounce your way down versus scrapping your way from the bottom up. But if you're already stuck and you're sensing a NO, or actually getting a NO at a lower level, I'd say find out why exactly the one you are with is at a NO (and don't let them sugarcoat it). Then maybe ask if there are others in the organization who might be able to use your services. Or you can decide to just go for it, and not worry about going over this person's head. But this can be a risky move depending on the nature of the relationship, your market place, your position in the market, or who this person is.

Q: *What if your main contact says he's sold, but just won't let you near the other people in the decision-making process to even make a presentation?*

A: The key there is that he "says he's sold." This is a common assumption we all make when selling. The reality is he's probably not sold at all and is either poisoning the well, or just not even telling anyone else about it. You must close the one you're with by proposing an action-oriented Mini-Step. If they take it, they may indeed be sold. If not, they're trying to tell you that either they're not sold, or they aren't willing to sell at the next level. Other than that, you can try to set up a meeting at the next level, or at least equip your contact to make a better presentation on your behalf. But chances are the answer is simple: Your contact isn't as sold as you believe him or her to be.

R E V I E W

• Just having the Mini-Steps isn't enough. You need to know how to ask good closing questions.

• When you have a defined Mini-Step, you can get more direct with your questioning through what we call an Assumptive Suggestion (an assumptive tone, but tempered with a suggestion).

• You must learn how to listen and respond to what you're hearing and seeing. Listening is actually observing, moving beyond the verbal, and focusing on the physical and action-steps.

• There are only two possible outcomes to an action-oriented question: Either YES the client is taking action, or NO the client is not taking action.

• If you get YES, seize the moment and be specific with your actions, and if you get affirmation, keep taking action steps.

• If you get NO, be realistic. Don't pretend you didn't see or hear the response given by the client.

• Mini-Steps are an excellent tool for closing various removed decision makers (RDMs) and lower-level decision makers (LLDMs).

Bonus Materials Available at the Online Resource Center:

• A streaming video segment from me on effective questioning, listening, observing and responding. (MP3 and written versions are available as well.)

CHAPTER 5

Embracing NO
as a Sales Culture

I make people better closers by helping them create Mini-Steps in the closing process, by teaching people how to ask better action-oriented questions, and by introducing them to "the dark side"—to the NO side of the equation—*early and often in the process.* I will guarantee you that if you will begin to accept, appreciate, and *embrace* NO within your sales culture, your life, your client's life, your sales manager's life—everyone's life—will become much more positive, productive and profitable! Seems odd to find a more *positive* outcome by embracing the *negative,* doesn't it. Well, it's just one of those wonderful surprises in life, and one of the reasons I think salespeople have been so drawn to my philosophies: *They are counter-culture to what every other salesperson on the street is doing.*

It's not that we as salespeople are unaware of NO. We know it exists, we've had people tell us NO, we've lost sales to NO. The problem is that we've never really *embraced* the concept early enough in the process, opting instead to wait till the close to be faced with the reality of NO (and even then we don't like to admit NO even exists: *"I lost it for now, boss, but I think they're coming back soon!"*). When I say *embrace,* I mean we don't value or hold up NO as a good answer to get in the sales process. We obviously embrace YES, and unfortunately we too often embrace MAYBE, but we are deathly afraid of hearing NO. We feel it's much more productive and positive to stay in Maybe-Land, than it is to venture into the scary world of NO.

WHAT I MEAN BY NO

When I use phrases like "embracing NO," "going to NO," and "taking people to NO," I'm speaking of NO as a mere resting point on the journey toward either YES . . . or NO FOREVER. So the phrase should really be NO-FOR-NOW, as in *"embracing NO-FOR-NOW," "going to NO-FOR-NOW,"* and *"taking clients to NO-FOR-NOW."*

NO Is Just a Resting Place: NO-FOR-NOW

Another way to look at NO is that it's the place the client sees in *his* head as we discuss doing business together, assuming he's not at a YES of course, for there are only two places to "be": either at YES, or at NO-FOR-NOW.

Let me use another example. Say that you're inviting me to a party (in which case you're the "salesperson" and I'm the "client"). I really don't want to go, but I'm going to be polite about it:

• The YES place is in your head (YES—I want you to come to the party)

- The NO place is in my head (NO—I don't want to go to the party)

- The Maybe-Land is that place in between YES and NO where we spend most of our time

Even though I'm thinking NO, I'll *say* things like, "I'll try to get over to your party," and you'll respond with, "Yeah, you really should. Do you think you'll be there?" And I may come back with, "Well, I'd like to go (polite lie), but we'll just have to see what else is going on."

The NO place is in *my* head. So if you want to go to the NO place, you just climb into my head and *call 'em as you see 'em.* By the way, you have to know HOW to go to the NO place so you don't come across as angry or defensive, and we'll cover all that in this chapter.

To climb into my NO head, you might say something like, "Greg, I appreciate you trying to get to the party, but for planning purposes it sounds honestly like you've decided not to come. And that's fine, we've got tons of other parties coming up." Once you climb into my head, and start speaking the reality I can't seem to muster, you'll start to make real progress.

Why do you think people dreamed up the R.S.V.P.? Because verbal acknowledgments and promises just couldn't be counted on. You either respond with a YES, or a NO. It defeats the purpose to respond with "Put us down for definite maybe." *Either you are coming or you are not, just respond, please, so we can do some planning.*

NO-FOR-NOW is just a resting place, designed to accomplish several tasks:

- To get rid of Maybe-Land, opting instead for NO-FOR-NOW. If salespeople and clients can see that NO-FOR-NOW is just a resting place, and that it doesn't have to be a life sentence, they'll more easily gravitate to using it.

  •   To get at negative issues that are never revealed in Maybe-Land. If we find out that someone is at a NO-FOR-NOW, and not a YES, we'll discover what the reasons are. Then we either deal with those issues and get on to YES, or discover that we can't deal with those issues and we move to a more permanent NO.

  •   NO-FOR-NOW is a flushing strategy to help keep our pipelines clean and flowing smoothly.

Going to NO-FOR-NOW is a powerful step, mainly because you're inside the client's mind, seeing reality and getting at core issues, many of which are negative and usually left unspoken. Which means it's going to be uncomfortable at first, just like with the R.S.V.P. For the person holding the party, it's nice for planning purposes to know who's going to be there. But if I'm the person responding, and especially if I am the type who when he didn't want to go had always given the ol' "I'll try to get over there," it means that when I respond with "NO, I won't be there," the question I have to be prepared to answer is, "Oh, okay. Why not?"

IF GOING TO NO (THE R.S.V.P.) MAKES SO MUCH SENSE, WHY DOESN'T EVERYONE IN SALES USE IT?

"I think going to NO is just unnatural for everyone—the salesperson, the client, and the sales manager," said Greg Brown, senior vice president of Sports at Learfield Sports, a client with whom I've been working for several years on, among other areas, embracing NO as a sales organization. He continued:

"Salespeople are classically trained over their careers to pursue a commitment, and *commitment* has always meant getting a YES. I mean, ultimately we're all trying to achieve a favorable commitment, but we've all come to realize that commitment can be a NO, and that NO is okay, and that it's far better than getting a 'maybe,' or a 'we're thinking about it,' or 'we're *very* interested.' And in the end, it's actually much better for the client too, because if they *think* NO, they're not going there by themselves. NO allows everyone to reset the table and clear the air, and it tells us exactly what needs to change in the future. This is so much better than everyone walking around in 'la-la land,' where the client thinks one thing and we think another. Meanwhile, we haven't done anything definitive to help determine where a particular client may or may not stand, except probably have another meeting and go through the same thing all over again."

Case Study: Learfield Sports

Since fully embracing NO as a culture, Learfield Sports has seen dramatic improvement in performance from the entire sales organization, including:

- Increased individual and overall sales
- Shorter sales cycles
- More long-term agreements
- Earlier renewals
- Greater customer satisfaction

We as salespeople are hard-wired and trained to get two possible answers: YES or MAYBE. Even if all the evidence tells you that what you're getting is a NO, it's more positive and productive to cover your ears and squint, and just pretend that what you're hearing and seeing is a YES or a MAYBE. With salespeople in all industries walking around with this as their mantra, it's easy to see where clients picked up the habit: If nearly all salespeople are wired to accept and even celebrate MAYBE, then that's what clients have learned to dole out to keep salespeople happy, and to get rid of them. So clients think, "If I only have two choices—YES or MAYBE—and I'm not at a YES, I guess I'm at a MAYBE."

These salespeople then become sales managers and eventually move into top sales management, where they train new salespeople, and thus the circle of life (or death, I should say) continues.

From sellers to managers to top management: When everyone is conditioned to accept only YES or MAYBE, embracing NO as a possible answer is going to take a top to bottom overhaul.

THE MUTUAL MYSTIFICATION LADDER

The deception and false stories start at the client level and work their way through the salesperson, to the sales manager, and all the way to the top of the organization. I call this the "Mutual Mystification Ladder." It starts with the client giving the salesperson a verbal MAYBE ("We're interested in maybe eventually doing something"), followed by the salesperson racing back to the office where the manager asks (essentially): "What did you get? A YES or a

MAYBE?" The salesperson, who wants to look good, feel good, or be a hero, says, "He said they're interested in eventually doing something." The manager, who also believes in YES or MAYBE as the only two answers, thinks, "Great . . . good job." The sales manager then reports this to the VP of Sales, who also believes in YES or MAYBE, and thinks, "Great . . . good job."

From client to seller, seller to sales manager, sales manager to top management—everyone is living in Maybe-Land, where we all look busy and productive, and where the outcomes *could be* wonderful.

Meanwhile, what everyone is avoiding is this little thing called REALITY. In Reality-World there are only two actual outcomes to any request: either YES or NO. No matter what I may say, either I showed up at the party, or I didn't.

THE 40 PERCENT GAP BETWEEN MAYBE-LAND AND REALITY-WORLD

I discovered the parallel worlds of MAYBE and NO and the *Mutual Mystification Ladder* through studying the sales pipelines and management accountability structures of thousands of salespeople, sales managers, and sales organizations over the past fifteen plus years. I basically looked at what the folks on the sales side of the equation were reporting as likely to "close" versus what the clients actually ended up doing. I discovered a gap between Maybe-Land and Reality-World of about 40 percent! Generally, salespeople believe that 70 percent of the prospects they put into their sales pipeline will become clients, when reality shows (based on informal research and study of sales pipelines and sales reports) that around 30 percent will end up as YES clients. This is a deadly gap that causes all sorts of havoc for clients, salespeople, and sales managers. We'll talk about some solutions later this chapter, and the one on managing consultative closing in Chapter 6.

For now, let's look at how the gap process actually happens in most sales offices:

- Salespeople are taught to look at each opportunity and asses the chances for a successful closing (remember, in their mind *closing* means only YES), and they then assign a *closing percentage guess* on each opportunity ("I think ABC Company is at a 50 percent chance of closing . . . XYZ is at 75 percent," etc.). As for how they come up with that number, it's usually nothing more than an educated guess, a "gut feel" (which is a major issue we deal with in Chapter 7). They will then list these opportunities on a weekly "Pending Report" that they turn in to the manager.

- Managers then keep an eye on these opportunities on a weekly basis as they move through the sales pipeline, maybe stopping long enough to ask salespeople about a few of the opportunities.

- As salespeople continue to work on the opportunities in the pipeline, they keep adjusting the percentage of close, either up or down, depending on their gut feel and on what the client may be doing.

- Eventually each opportunity either closes for a YES, ends up a NO, or just sort of sits and festers as a MAYBE until the seller just doesn't list it anymore.

When we look at the difference between what is reported, and what actually happened, one thing is very clear: NO is a much more prevalent outcome than salespeople or sales managers want to accept or acknowledge. So if in reality there are more NOs in the pipeline, it stands to reason that these NOs didn't suddenly come at the last minute. They were probably NOs for a long time; in fact, many of them should have never been in the pipeline to begin with because they really weren't potential clients.

The question then becomes, why do salespeople want to put nonqualified prospects in the pipeline, and then keep them there pretending they have more potential than they really do. I mean, if we're having a party, wouldn't it make sense to invite people we want to come, and who have potential for being able to come, and then send out R.S.V.P.s so that we'll know who's coming and can plan accordingly?. Seems logical to apply the same thought process to our sales life, doesn't it?

Well, sales is much more involved and complicated than planning a dinner party. When you're talking sales, you're talking money, careers, ancient roles being played out in a strange play—plus all sorts of emotional and psychological inner and outer games we all play, between client and seller, seller and manager, and manager and top manager.

If I can boil it down for the sake of keeping it simple, here are the main reasons why I think sellers would rather have a pipeline full of MAYBEs than one full of YES's or NO-FOR-NOWs:

• Even though it's a false sense of security, it makes me feel good to have lots of "things happening." It's nicer to think I've got thirty good prospects in the pipeline, than to face the truth and discover that only four are real.

• If I have all these potentially hot deals, why do I have to invest time in prospecting for new ones? *Because I really HATE prospecting, I'd rather just pretend that every-*

thing is real. "Call Reluctance" is at the heart of most prospecting issues, and prospecting issues are at the heart of most closing issues. We'll address both topics in Chapter 7.

• I want a good story to share in my pending report each week. I can't very well give my manager a sheet with just two or three deals on it. I'd rather baffle her and give her MAYBEs; that way I know she'll never be able to track it from week to week and I can fly beneath the radar.

• Plus, I think that if I can just keep clients at MAYBE and "Interested," I can push them over the edge to YES.

Even though salespeople feel they can save some sales by keeping them on life support, I think the main reason they won't get a true read on client's intentions early on in the process is that they don't really *want* to know reality. They don't want to ask . . . because they don't want to know. For that "knowing" could mean a negative response, which could lead to an early exit from the pending report, which would mean they'd have to be replaced, which would mean having to prospect for new people, which would mean dealing with fear, rejection, starting over, and so on, and so on.

ALL MADE POSSIBLE BY YOUR FRIENDS AT THE VERBAL TWO-STEP PROCESS

The reason the gap between Maybe-Land and Reality-World can exist is because most people are selling from a verbal-only, two-step process. This is why Mini-Steps and Embracing NO will always work together. Neither can really work without the other, for if you have Mini-Steps broken out and you're accepting MAYBE as an answer, the steps do little good. And if you're Embracing NO, but you've got no action steps to ask for YES or NO, then you'll be just as ineffective.

When there are defined and understood (between client and seller, seller and manager) Mini-Steps in the process, then we can put an end to the Mutual Mystification Ladder, and the entire concept of salespeople "guessing" what a hypothetical closing percentage may be. Instead, we're going to just look at our R.S.V.P.s: We're going to, in a sense, let the clients tell us where they are in the pipeline based on their action, or lack of action.

NOW THAT WE HAVE MINI-STEPS IN THE PROCESS, WE MUST EMBRACE NO

The presence of Mini-Steps in the process is designed to create more direct closing questions, which in turn should lead to more closing opportunities. And because *closing* means YES *or* NO, we're bound to have more NOs emerging. And since we'll have more NOs, we'd better learn to embrace the answer—and learn how to deal with it when it comes—as part of our process for making things happen. This is much, much easier said than done.

In my years of one-on-one coaching, nothing has been harder than getting salespeople comfortable embracing NO as a good answer. Even though they've been through training and have heard all my reasons why NO is better than MAYBE, they still feel NO is *evil,* that it is the "anti-sale," scary, a life sentence they can't recover from.

This to me is very sad, because for those who've tried it, and who now swear by it, will tell you that embracing

NO as an answer is the single most liberating, fun, and productive thing they've ever done! And, as an added bonus, they'll report that clients *actually like them more, the more they bring up the word NO as a possible answer.*

We've covered why salespeople are comfortable with MAYBE, but let's look at the other side:

Why Salespeople Are So Afraid of NO

• ***They've done a lot of work to get a client to a certain point and don't want to blow it.*** They've probably spent a great deal of time prospecting and working their way in to an opportunity with a client, they've questioned and probed, they've listened and presented ideas, and they probably developed several proposals along the way. It's too hard to imagine just saying NO and walking away.

• ***They feel that NO is too final and MAYBE is a more comfortable resting place.*** When we were kids asking our parents whether we could spend the night at a friend's house, we'd be excited about hearing a "maybe." It wasn't a NO, and it meant the momentum would probably carry us to a YES (especially if we could play mom's MAYBE on dad). But a sales call is much different. We're dealing with a different animal here: A client who is actively engaged in his role within a sales call, the sales clock is on, and the word MAYBE usually leads to anything but a YES. In fact, MAYBE usually leads to a stalled sale, a covering up of the real issues, and eventually a NO, whether it's said or the thing just sort of "goes away."

• ***They like to be liked and don't want to cause conflict.*** I feel this is a big one, and it impacts a lot of salespeople: Most people just don't like to admit it. People tell me all the time in workshops or seminars:

"I don't care about being liked."

"I don't mind the conflict part of it . . . I LIKE conflict."

Sorry, I don't buy it. That sounds cool, and macho, and so very rebellious to say in front of peers in a workshop, but it's a different thing when it's just the salesperson and the client one-on-one, away from the glare of anyone else. I think down deep we all like to be liked and accepted, and we don't like to be thought of as the man or woman who creates conflict for the client. Salespeople find it's much easier, faster, and less stressful to accept the client's MAYBE bone they toss their way than to face what they feel is the harsh reality of NO.

• *They like having a good story to tell their boss, partner, friend, spouse—and mostly, themselves.* I like to ask managers, "How many salespeople come back from a sales call and say, 'That sucked . . . there is no potential . . . zero possibility'?" They all laugh because they know the opposite is true. Salespeople usually come back with some sort of positive spin:

"This one is going to be big."

"Well, I think it could eventually turn into something."

"Nothing now, but a ton of potential, I think."

Whether it's ego, or pride, or a desire only to see positive outcomes, whatever the reason, we all like to tell ourselves and others good stories about how things are going, what we've got cookin', and how we've got our act together. While it's beautiful to believe in a positive outcome, it's nuts to look at the reality of today and just pretend that a NO client is really a YES client.

EMBRACING NO IS GOOD FOR THE CLIENT

I have found there are many opposites in the world of sales, where reality is opposite of our perception, and the embracing of NO is one of these opposites. The general perception is that "going to NO" is going to cause conflict and harm the relationship with the client, when the exact opposite is usually true. When we acknowledge the ugly NO elephant in the room, the client is usually relieved because we're saying things they're thinking, but can't express. *Thus they end up liking us more!*

When we're in the role of client (the one being pursued), and we're not excited about a relationship, it's funny how we'll encourage the salesperson (the pursuer) to do the one thing we don't want them to do: pursue us. Instead of saying, "I don't want you to call on me again. I will never buy this service," we say, "I don't have anything now, but maybe in the future. Why don't you stay in touch? We may end up doing something." As we've covered, we practice this art of subtle deception in order to spare the feelings of the salesperson, and to avoid potential conflict. However, while it's true we're avoiding the conflict of that moment, we're setting ourselves up for future conflict when the salesperson takes our advice and *stays in touch* with calls, proposals, and new ideas. What is amazing in this little scenario is that we get *mad at salespeople* for taking our advice.

I believe when a client is feeling negatively about a salesperson or the product, he really wants the salesperson to "take a hint" and go to the place she just can't or *won't* go: the *"It's a NO"* place. And when the salesperson does take care of that *dirty work,* the client actually ends up liking her more, and ironically (again, lots of opposites in sales), he may be *more* favorable to giving her future business.

So am I suggesting that—with a client who is really at a NO but is stuck in MAYBE—the easier we make it to say NO, the more likely we are to get YES? *Exactly!* It may sound crazy, but it's true. I've personally experienced the phenomenon hundreds of times, and have taught it successfully to salespeople, managers, and business owners; many of whom have returned years later to tell me that *going to NO is the most powerful thing they were taught about forming relationships while closing.*

I've had several conversations with clients about this "going to NO" concept and how they feel about it within the sales process. The comments I get are pretty consistent, usually sounding like:

• I like the fact that someone is dealing in reality, even if the reality is we're not going to be working together on this project.

• I'm never as positive as I pretend to be in a sales call, and I appreciate salespeople so much more who recognize where it's not a fit and just call it that. I'm more likely to buy something from them in the future just because of that honesty.

• It's not easy telling people NO. I try to demonstrate to salespeople when I have no interest in a product, but they rarely want to go there. They'd rather leave with a lukewarm MAYBE and then keep calling and bugging me.

WHEN TO USE NO WITHIN THE SALES PROCESS

Remember, there are only two possible outcomes to a direct action-oriented ask: YES, the client is taking action, or NO, the client is not taking action. The world of *MAYBE the client will take action* is only a fantasy world salespeople and clients have dreamed up to avoid reality. So the time to "use" NO is whenever you don't get a YES answer—for what other place is there to go but NO? Nothing else exists.

The difference is that we're very conditioned and very comfortable going to MAYBE when we don't get YES, and I'm saying we must go to NO instead. Why? As stated before (and important to repeat over and over again): in NO we get at issues and concerns. In MAYBE we get platitudes and promises.

Here are some of the times it would make sense to "go to NO" (we'll talk about *how* we do it below):

• When you've asked a client to take a small or large Mini-Step and he stalls, is evasive, makes excuses why he can't.

• When a client looks at a proposal for any length of time, and won't give you an answer.

• When you're trying to get more information about another decision maker and the client isn't forthcoming with details, or won't allow you access to a meeting.

• When you're asking for the client's help in the process (gathering more information, getting access to past history, finding out about budgets or buying criteria) *and you're generally getting pushback in any area.*

• When your client is suddenly evasive: He won't call you back, won't answer e-mails, seems nervous when you talk.

• When a client suddenly introduces new "rules of the game": new buyers in the process, new budget parameters, new hurdles to jump over, new tasks to wait for.

Going to NO is something we have to be comfortable using at any time in a sales relationship with a client. It could be in the first 5 minutes of a call and I'm getting tremendous pushback or resistance, or it could be midway through our process after the client has taken 10 of my 20 Mini-Steps. Of course it can also happen toward the latter stages, when we're asking for more committed closing steps.

Again, just because I'm going to NO doesn't mean I intend to stay there. It is a strategic move designed to jolt the client out of the neutral zone and get at the underlying reality.

However, we have to be careful how we go to NO; there are certain body language skills and verbal strategies we must employ in order to continue to build relationships rather than tearing them down.

HOW TO "GO TO NO" WITHOUT HURTING THE RELATIONSHIP

When we start asking clients to leave the fantasy world of MAYBE and take us into the darker "underworld" of NO, we have to do it in a way that doesn't alarm or offend them. We're basically traveling inside their mind, to where the true reality of a situation lies, and we have to "go there" in a way that is comfortable for both parties. We must remember that clients aren't used to having this type of conversation with salespeople.

All of our communication—body language as well as verbal language and tone—must be carefully controlled and scripted as we introduce NO into the situation.

What We Say When Going to NO

• I like to start with a *softener* to help ease in the question. Here are a few of the *softener phrases* I use:

"Out of curiosity. . . ." (I find you can say anything to people once you say, "*Out of curiosity. . . .*")

"I get the sense that. . . ."

"I have this *gut feeling* that. . . ." (Not exactly "soft," but it works.)

•   Next, I will assume there are issues—or problems or concerns—that must be causing the problems:

> "Out of curiosity, Mr. Client, it sounds like there are some concerns you have with what we've proposed to this point. . . ."

•   I will then do a concept I call: *"Fishin' in the Ugly Pond"* (I'll explain the concept in more detail in a moment), which is basically saying a negative thing I think may be one of the "issues" the client has:

> "Out of curiosity, Mr. Client, it sounds like there are some concerns you have with what we've proposed to this point. I sense that it has something to do with the return on investment, is that correct?"

> (The client will typically either agree with that negative, or see it as a green light to give me additional negatives—which is a GOOD thing, not a bad thing.)

•   Finally, I will take the issues we've identified and make an assumption that the client has decided not to move forward, that they're at a *NO-FOR-NOW:*

> "Out of curiosity, Mr. Client, it sounds like there are some concerns you have with what we've proposed to this point. I sense that it has something to do with the return on investment, is that correct? (Client agrees or adds more issues.) And I'm also

sensing (a softener tossed in there again) that this is a big enough issue to cause you be at a 'NO-for-now.' How accurate is that?"

Body Language When Going to NO

Our body language is something we have to consciously control at certain times within the sales call, particularly when going to the NO side of the equation (because of the potential conflict that could happen).

Here are a few suggestions:

• When initially making the move to "go negative," I suggest you make some change in your overall posture, such as leaning forward or back, folding or unfolding your legs, etc.

• Signal that you are "backing off" somehow, either by turning notepad over or closing it. If you have a presentation of a proposal you're working through, you might turn it over or pull it back towards you.

• To show that you're NOT defensive about the client telling you ugly things, make sure your face is not contorting in strange ways, or that you're not suddenly nodding your head or shaking it back and forth too quickly. Don't send signals like, "Fine, fine. No, that's great . . . just GREAT. I've been working on this for three months and THIS is what I get?"

Controlling our body language and reading the body language of our clients are skill sets every salesperson should at least explore and perhaps master. If our goal is to create deeper, more profitable long-term relationships, we should be at least have a working knowledge of how humans act and react nonverbally during a call.

Fishin' in the Ugly Pond

The concept of "Fishin' in the Ugly Pond" is something I developed years ago to describe what happens when the salesperson takes the lead and starts bringing up what *could be* potential negatives (ugly fish) the client may be feeling or thinking. I say *may be feeling* because we're just not sure—thus the term "fishin'." But even if we're wrong, it's okay, because we're sending a signal to the client that says, "We can obviously hear negative things because we're the ones bringing them up . . . so fire away."

Here's what this move sounds like:

SALESPERSON (after leaning back and turning over the proposal): "Ms. Client, this is just a guess on my part (another softener), but my sense is that you've decided NOT to go with our product, and that the main reason is you're just not comfortable with our service options. Is that correct?"

CLIENT: "Well, yeah. I think that's part of it. It's also. . . . " (Client will most likely take your cue and add a few negatives of her own.)

Clients aren't used to a salesperson wanting this much honesty (and remember, they're not comfortable with conflict), so it may take some coaxing to get it out of them.

Here are some pointers for improving your *fishin'*:

• Bring up challenge areas that the client has expressed, or that your gut is telling you they're feeling. Don't introduce new problem areas.

• Be a bit skeptical if the client mentions money, or timing, as their negatives: Those are usually smoke screens for deeper issues. If you get one of these, say something like, "I appreciate that, Ms. Client. However, I'm sensing some other issues, because even if you HAD the money (or HAD the time), I don't think you're ready to move forward with our company. How accurate is that?"

BRINGING A CLIENT BACK FROM NO

NO may be the final answer from the client, and that's fine; at least they're out of the pipeline and I can stop stalking them. Often, however, NO is merely a "flushing point," where I can hear the issues keeping us from ever working together. Sometimes these NO issues can be dealt with and the client can be turned around, especially if the reasons they give have to do with wrong information, or incorrect assumptions on their part.

When the issues are the type we feel we can address and possibly turn the client around, here is a process for going through NO and heading back to YES:

• We must get out of the Neutral Zone and officially go to NO (because we obviously can't go to YES, and we must do one or the other):

SALESPERSON: "So just to be clear, we're really at a NO, at least for now. . . ." (Expect the client to fight this as you're going opposite and their instinct is to fight you.)

• Do something to signal a break in the action: Turn over your notebook, or close your proposal. "Game off. . . ."

• Lean back and pause a moment.

• Thank the client for his honesty: "I appreciate you being honest with me. . . ."

• Let the client know it will HELP YOU to hear the truth, even if it's ugly: "It would help me tremendously if you could share the issues that are causing you to be at NO. . . ."

• Be skeptical if they soft-pedal on the answer: "I know bad timing is part of it. However, my sense is that there is something more, another concern you have. . . ."

• Once you snag the main concern, have the client go into as much detail as possible:

> "So really, Mr. Client, the issue has to do with the fact that we don't offer free roaming outside of our four-state region. Can you talk specifically about why this is SUCH a concern?"

• Let the client talk without you firing back with come-back answers, like "But let me explain why. . . ."

• After the client goes into detail on which issue is causing you to be at NO-FOR-NOW, it's time for a strategy I call "Going to the Movies."

GOING TO THE MOVIES

Going to the Movies involves playing mental movies with the client, so you can get an idea of what they're seeing as they imagine buying your product or service. There are two movies you can watch: a bad movie, where the client imagines owning your product or service and the bad things that can happen, and a good movie, where the client imagines owning your product or service and the good things that can happen. *A client at NO typically only owns the bad movie, and they watch it over and over again as you try to present your solutions and deal with their concerns.*

• You start by playing the only movie they own (the bad one), and you describe what you're seeing as if you were sitting on the couch next to the client. Describe what they must be going through (be as brutally honest as you like):

SALESPERSON: "So it sounds like what you see happening is this: You decide to go with our company. You're happy with the monthly savings, but then some people are mad because they're paying for roaming, and you have to defend your decision. Is that right?"

• You'll find that clients often nod their heads up and down in agreement as you play the bad movie. *This is a critical bonding moment* as you are deep within their world, seeing what they're seeing, envisioning what they're envisioning. They've never had a salesperson this committed to hearing the TRUE reality, especially when that reality is negative. This is Consultative Closing at it's very best. In many cases, clients will continue the movie with even more bad images:

CLIENT: "Yeah, you're right. And we're in a real budget cutting mood right now, so I can't be wasting money. . . ."

• Now that you're sitting on the couch watching their ugly movie, you've earned the right and the emotional standing to introduce another possibility: the good movie. In this movie, the client buys the product or service and the outcome is good. *The client at this NO stage probably doesn't own this video:*

SALESPERSON: "Well, I can see why you wouldn't be happy with that outcome, but let me ask you something (softener and a turn to positive). Let me ask you this: Let's say you decide to go with our service, and you introduce it. Some folks are a little nervous about the roaming, but they see that the everyday charges are much less and there are fewer dropped calls, which in their mind makes up for the extra fees when roaming. Plus the roaming fees actually encourage people to use their phones much more efficiently when traveling. What would your thoughts be?"

• Remember, clients don't own the good video. It's an outcome they've never imagined, and it's going to take some getting used to. Usually they'll stop nodding their heads up and down and get an uncertain look on their face. Maybe the eyebrows will flash up and down along with a quick head twitch, as if thinking, "Well, I GUESS it could work. Who knows . . . that WOULD be a nice outcome."

• Soon however, reality comes back and they'll say something like:

CLIENT: "Well, yeah, that WOULD be nice, but I'm not sure it would happen."

• I love this next move because it really cuts to the chase:

SALESPERSON: "I understand. But what if it DID work like I've just described, you'd HAVE to go with it, wouldn't you?"

• You now have at least two possible outcomes where there was just one moments ago. And your job is to acknowledge both movies as you attempt to get the client back on track toward a YES outcome. I personally like the "LET'S DO THIS" approach to reconciling the situation:

SALESPERSON: "Let's do this (acknowledge their bad thoughts). I know you're still a bit nervous about how the roaming fees will be received (now a hop to the good video), but at the same time you're excited about the day-in and day-out savings, and at least a 40 percent reduction in dropped calls. Let's do this: I'm going to recommend you make the switch to our service, and that I will work with you closely on a monthly basis to analyze the long-distance roaming charges to make sure they're in line, and I'll help you get that information out to your troops in the field. I will also help you structure some materials that will show clearly why you made the decision to switch to our firm. (Go for a Mini-Step.) Let's at least. . . ."

•   If you continue to get pushback from the client there are two things that could have happened:

1. Your *good movie* just wasn't strong enough to overcome the *bad movie*, and until it is, you'll never make that sale.

2. Your good movie was better than the bad movie, but the bad movie issues weren't the real problem to begin with. Until you can get at the core problem areas, you'll never make that sale.

EMBRACING NO THROUGHOUT THE SALES DEPARTMENT

One of the rules I institute as part of my overall work with clients in creating "The Ultimate Sales Organization" (which is a series of fifteen core disciplines you'll find on my blog: http://GregBennett.blogs.com):

> Salespeople will hold client's accountable to the direct
> degree sales managers hold salespeople accountable.
> If managers accept MAYBE, salespeople will accept
> MAYBE.

I believe at the core of most closing problems is the fact that there is no one to help the salesperson, professional, or business owner—whoever is doing the selling—to face the reality of a particular sales situation. The client sells the salesperson on accepting MAYBE, the salesperson sells the manager on accepting MAYBE, and the sales manager sells top management and owners of the business on accepting MAYBE.

What if we all magically found out the true reality about the world of MAYBE: that it's really a disguised NO, and that, while making us feel better and more secure on the sales side, it was actually causing lots of hidden damage not only to our potential sales, but to the client and our possible long-term relationship? If we somehow could know that, and could see it, would we still be so excited to race to MAYBE? I don't think so.

I'd much rather have a clear picture of where clients and potential clients truly are in their decision-making process when they think of using my services. How do they REALLY feel? What are the true core issues that must be addressed before we would ever get to YES?

See, I think it's much healthier to be able to go down your prospect list and speak about the reality of the situation:

• *ABC Alliance.* Is at a NO-FOR-NOW. The main issues are price of our Gold Service and lack of guarantee.

No Mini-Steps taken as of yet. I will overcome by continuing to work on adding value and assurances after the sale.

   •   *DEF Partners.* Is at a NO-FOR-NOW. Issues are their main supplier has the contract through end of the year, and thereafter has first rights of refusal to match offers. Main supplier may be in trouble and have to shut down prior to that, however. Main Mini-Step I've taken is to get a conditional agreement to go with us, should this supplier drop out.

   •   *GHI Group.* Is at a NO-FOR-NOW. Waiting for final approval of budget. I have taken three early Mini-Steps. Will be a YES by end of the month

   These clients are at a NO-FOR-NOW. That's reality. If they're not at a YES, they're at a NO-FOR-NOW. I emphasize "FOR NOW" because, it's just for *now*–this minute, and every minute up to the point of becoming a YES.

   Now contrast this with the typical Maybe-Land, pending list that salespeople turn in to management:

   •   *ABC Alliance.* Is looking pretty good. Working up a new proposal and will meet with key people next week. I'd say a 70 percent chance of eventually doing something.

   •   *DEF Partners.* Could be big. They have an agreement now, but they like us and said they'd consider using us in the future if the main supplier craps out. It's, say, 80 percent if they crap out.

   •   *GHI Group.* Definitely a go, or at least close. Just waiting for some last minute things to come through.

   What are the three main differences about the two lists?

1. The second list (Maybe-Land List) is written by someone trying to sell themselves and sell management on how good something looks, by listing the positives and lightly guessing at the negatives.

2. The first list is much clearer in the language used, especially when describing what clients DON'T like, and what issues are blocking the way.

3. The first list mentions the Mini-Steps taken, which should give the manager a more realistic and clear view of where the client truly is, *not where the rose-colored-glasses-wearing salesperson says he is.*

Here is the main difference between MAYBE and NO: As a salesperson, if I believe MAYBE is the same as YES, *I'll stop working hard and start counting on the sale* (which means I'll also stop looking for new prospects to add to the funnel). If, however, I believe MAYBE is the same as NO-FOR-NOW, *I'll start working harder to identify the issues and addressing them until I get complete closure* (YES or NO), and I'll keep on prospecting because until something is 100 percent done, it's a NO.

SOME FREQUENTLY ASKED QUESTIONS ABOUT EMBRACING NO

Q: *Aren't you bringing up negatives that may not be there, or highlighting them too much?*

A: I can see how it may appear that way, especially when we're as focused (as we are in this chapter) on the NO side of the equation, but in reality when the NO side is worked in with the YES side, it's not as dramatic as it seems. I usually don't have to go to an extreme to come up with negatives on the part of the client. I find they're always there, swimming just beneath the surface in the Ugly Pond. We're just not used to talking about them. Clients would rather keep those things hidden and just talk about what they like about us.

Q: *What if a client agrees with you and goes right to NO?*

A: Great! NO is one of two really good answers to get in sales—YES or NO—because they're actually the only two answers that exist. When I get NO, I can find out reasons we're at NO, and either turn those reasons around right there, or at least know what would have to change in the future for us to ever do business together. When your car is stuck in the snow, and you're at the bottom of the rut, you can't just keep hitting the gas, hoping to go forward. Sometimes you've got to go in reverse, then forward again, then reverse. Anything but being stuck in NEUTRAL is good—at least you're moving. A worst-case scenario is the client is at NO, I can't turn them, at least I'm not stalking them, and they're not clogging my pipeline. *NEXT!*

Q: *Isn't talking about NO very negative? I believe in being optimistic with a client, but is that possible when you're always mentioning NO?*

A: This is one of those "opposites" I've discovered in sales. You would think that bringing up negative thoughts and ideas would make you less likeable by the client, but the exact opposite usually happens: They end up LOVING you! I think it's mainly because when you start talking about what a client may not like about your product or service, you're dealing in reality. It's what they feel, but can't express, and for that they'll like you and respect you. I've only found it to be a liberating and very positive experience IF—and it's a big IF—the process is done right and you are genuine in your desire to solve needs and propose only what works for the client.

Remember: Embracing NO is good for the customer, good for the salesperson, and good for the entire sales organization.

REVIEW

- NO is just a resting place. It's NO-FOR-NOW.

- NO is designed to get rid of Maybe-Land because MAYBE is so hard to move clients out of. When we get NO, we get reasons, and when we get reasons, we have a chance to bring the client back to YES.

- The Mutual Mystification Ladder is the chain of deception that starts with the client being deceptive to the salesperson, and the salesperson then being deceptive to the manager, and then the manager being deceptive to top management.

- We must learn how to "go to NO" and "Fish in the Ugly Pond" in order to get at the ugly feelings and thoughts that are swimming beneath the client's surface

- In order to get back to YES, the salesperson must learn how to go all the way into NO, and then "Go to the Movies" with the client, watching both the bad movie the client is seeing, and introducing a competing good movie.

Bonus Materials Available at the Online Resource Center:

    • A streaming video role-play, with me "Going to NO" with a client and bringing them back to YES. (An MP3 and a written transcript of the role-play are also available.)

CHAPTER 6

Consultative Closing by Focusing on *After the Sale*

I can make anyone a better closer by focusing not only on simple steps that happen before the sale happens—after we've laid out our Mini-Steps and closing plan and learned to accept only YES or NO as an answer—but on *after* the sale, when the client is ready to take ownership of the newly purchased product or service. This is an area that is TOTALLY ignored by almost everyone in sales, and not just by the sleazy sales types, but even by the more consultative salespeople who go out of their way to focus on building solid relationships! And this lack of execution on the "after sale" has a major impact on closing before the sale.

I believe the problem lies in poor execution of the consultative sales model. Consultative selling is supposed to be all about merging the two sides of the sales equation (the "before the sale" and "after the sale," as well as the roles of salesperson on one side and client on the other) into one seamless process, so the salesperson and client are *partnered together* from the beginning to identify needs, determine solutions, and share in the long-term rewards as the needs of both sides are met. In this type of selling, the salesperson ideally should be involved as much *after* the sale as *before*. And not just on the initial sale: The partnership should extend long into the future with additional work and countless referrals flowing to the salesperson.

While the *concept* is great, and every consultative salesperson should certainly buy into it, *our execution is terrible.* And the problem areas are pretty easy to identify, and luckily pretty easy to fix with some more of my simple steps.

The problem starts with a lack of "after the sale" structure, or what exactly happens after the client "takes ownership" and is counting on working with the salesperson to *maximize their investment* in the product or service. I want to emphasize that I didn't write *"to use"* the product or service. We need to do more than show someone how to use it, we need to *partner with clients* to help them MAXIMIZE THEIR INVESTMENT IN OUR PRODUCT OR SERVICE. This lack of structure and process is similar to the other areas of sales we've addressed in this book, where Mini-Steps give tangible structure to the sales pursuit and pipeline processes. What I'm talking about is doing the same thing in the follow-up process.

The reality in nearly every sales organization I've ever worked in, consulted with, or experienced as a buyer, is that we pretty much all do the same thing: We do a great job of wooing the client—putting on our best duds, looking sharp, being attentive, and acting super sweet . . . UNTIL the client buys. Then everything changes. Just as the client is taking ownership, the salesperson and the salesperson's company pretty much "leave the building," or at least become scarce and less attentive and sweet. This leaves the client trying to figure out what they're doing and usually flailing around creating nominal results.

I'm not saying that everyone acts this way, or that we

don't *try* to provide service and follow-up—many companies provide great customer service. I'm just saying that for the most part (and I think we all have to be honest about this and not defensive) we don't act the same AFTER the client buys compared to how we acted BEFORE they bought. Even if we're calling ourselves consultative salespeople, who take great pride in our *customer-centric* and *value-added* approach, all of us range from "just okay" to "really terrible" in the after-the-sale" areas.

I have gotten into many arguments with managers and business owners, who challenge me on this when I do public workshops or seminars. They'll come up and say, "Greg, you're making a big assumption there. We think we do a great job after the sale and we certainly don't ignore the client." And I'll say, "Great, good for you. Do you mind if I ask you a few questions?" I will then ask them to explain in detail their post-buy process and how it works, including the set meetings they have, their proactive plan to maximize the investment, and a few other steps I recommend. Of course, very few have much to come back with besides something like, "Well, we have a customer service department, and I definitely encourage our sellers to stay in the client's face, answering any questions and solving any problems when they come up."

And I'll assure them that that is GREAT. There's nothing "wrong" with it, it's typical for a good company, but it's just not what I'm talking about when I'm talking about forming a partnership with the client to maximize their investment. When they "get it" and see the simple steps—how they work to not only dramatically improve customer service but also help in the closing process—the lights go on and we start to make some real headway.

The good news in all of this is that every other salesperson and sales organization you're competing against is equally as terrible (probably worse), but you're the one reading this book, and you're the one who will be able to follow these simple steps for dramatically improving the After-the-Sale portion of the sales process and forming better long-term relationships than anyone else in your market.

Let's start with some basic, common sense assumptions:

- Salespeople care about themselves and their needs more than they care about the client's.

- Clients care about themselves and their needs more than they care about the salesperson's.

I'm not saying we don't love clients, and we may even care deeply about them, but the reality is, unless we're Gandhi or Mother Theresa (and some of you may be), we generally put our needs, and the needs of our family and friends, over those of other people. And assuming that is true, it means that:

- Salespeople are going to care more about what happens BEFORE the sale.

- Clients are going to care more about what happens AFTER the sale.

Again, it's okay. It's only natural. For example, the salesperson inside a big-screen-TV store is excited and focused generally on what happens inside her store BEFORE the customer buys: How do the displays look and sound? How does she personally look and sound? Does she know the features and benefits of each model? Does she know the prices? How much does she need to sell to make her bonus? Or where is she in sales for the month? Meanwhile, the customer is excited about what happens AFTER the TV leaves the store and enters his family room and is plugged in. Sure, the salesperson will provide plenty of resources for the client, if there is a problem after he gets home. But chances are, she's not going to call the customer next week and ask, "Well, did you enjoy watching the *Star Wars Trilogy* as much as you thought you would? What else have you been watching?"

THE DIFFERENCE IN HOW SALESPEOPLE AND CLIENTS VIEW THE SALES PROCESS

Years ago when I was in the radio advertising sales business, I noticed the dramatic difference between the way I, and most other salespeople, treated the clients before the sale versus the way we treated them after the sale.

As an eager salesperson I focused all my energies and my station's resources on "getting the sale," which in that case meant getting the client on the air. I produced slick presentation pieces, developed colorful proposals on PowerPoint, and even wrote and recorded several "spec" ads—all to excite the client and get him to buy.

Once he bought, the story was different. Just as he was getting all excited to be "on the air" (something he had built into a magnificent thing and I treated like an everyday occurrence), I was traipsing off to the next kill. And what the client saw AFTER the sale, if I gave him anything at all, wasn't like the beautiful presentation pieces I did BE-FORE the sale; after the sale he *maybe* would get a beat-up cassette with his ad on it, marked with a label stuck on top of ten labels from other clients. That's it!

Another thing he didn't get, and this really speaks to the heart of what Consultative Closing is all about, is an "owner's manual" for how to maximize his investment with my radio station. I just assumed he knew what to do once he bought the ad. I figured he'd know what to put in the ad, how to make the ad effective, how to capture names of people who called or stopped in, how to sell the customers and then get them on the store mailing list, and so forth. Well, I was wrong. The client knew how to do *some* things inside his own store, but he was clueless about the rest. And our attitude at the station was, *"Our job is to run ads and bring 'em in . . . your job is to sell 'em."*

While that's a catchy little slogan, it's ridiculously shortsighted on the part of the salesperson and the station. Because when that client tries to use the product on his own and it doesn't work, he's not going to blame himself, *HE'S GOING TO BLAME ME!* And he *should* blame me, because I did very little to assure he'd be successful after he took ownership.

I realized early on that I could greatly increase my closing ratios, and develop much deeper relationships with clients at the same time, if I simply paid attention to what happens AFTER they own my product, with at least as much as, if not more than, of the "what's it gonna take to get you in this baby" BEFORE-the-Sale mindset.

I then began to create more tangible After-the-Sale Mini-Steps that I could highlight and actually schedule as part of my Before-the-Sale selling process.

It wasn't long after starting my training career in 1988 that I realized how many other salespeople and sales organizations operate the exact same way: focusing almost all their time, effort, and resources on getting the sale in the door, and not providing much to clients after the sale to help them maximize their investment.

I believe there are several reasons why salespeople don't focus on the After-the-Sale process:

*   ***They are afraid to hear the results.*** What if they do a follow-up meeting and the client is upset because it's not working? It's easier to just keep quiet and hope for the best.

*   ***They're not really sure how to help the client maximize their purchase.*** I'm shocked at how few businesses teach their salespeople how to really use the things they're out there selling! I mean we spend a good deal of time, energy, and money on teaching salespeople about the features and benefits of a product, but very little on the various ways this product should be used to solve problems for clients. It would be like teaching doctors only about medicines and cool pieces of medical equipment, but not teaching them about the various diseases that are out there, how to diagnose those maladies, and then how to match solutions to the problems.

*   ***They are interested primarily in their own well-being.*** This goes back to the earlier common sense assumptions we made. We're all pretty self absorbed, and can get too "inside" our own industry. And this includes clients, too! I think we forget that clients are just as self-centered as we are, but the burden is on us: If we want to form a relationship with our clients, *we need to focus on the things they focus on,* namely their well-being. Of course, this is nothing new. Dale Carnegie said it years ago, and I'm paraphrasing now: "You get what you want by getting people what *they* want."

- ***They're compensated on getting the "next kill":***
Once they've made the sale, they're on to the next one with
no time to turn around and make sure the client is maximizing the investment. This is what they're compensated to do:
*You get 20 percent for a new client, then 5 percent on every-
thing else he buys in the future.* The signal this sends? Go
get new business and do just enough to keep 'em on board
after they buy. And I don't think there's necessarily anything wrong with this approach, because it IS important to
keep hunting down new business, but I wonder sometimes
how things would be different for follow-up if salespeople
got the same or even more of a percentage from a *repeat*
customer as from a new one. (*You get 15 percent for a new
customer, and 20 percent after that for everything else they
buy.*) I wonder if in the end we wouldn't all be better off
taking care of existing customers, because we know they'll
continue to buy. Also, they'll kick lots of referrals our way,
and referrals are a hell of a lot easier to close than cold
contacts.

Because the mindset of self over others *is* so ingrained
in both sides of the sales process, we're not going to magically change it overnight. But we don't have to change the
world completely to make a major impact. If we want to
separate ourselves from the competition, we just have to focus
a bit more on the other side's needs and wake up to the fact
that we need to develop better strategies and processes for
the After-the-Sale process.

ALL WE HAVE TO DO TO IMPROVE IS FOCUS MORE ON AFTER THE SALE

The subtitle of this book says "Simple Steps," and these are
very simple steps you can make today to improve your

short-term closing and long-term relationships. All we're going to do is elevate our "After-the-Sale" process so that clients feel more secure in their purchase and improve their chances for a good ROI (return on investment).

And I'm talking really, really simple steps here, folks, so there is no excuse NOT to get these into place right way.

Step 1: Create a "Maximizer Manual" for Everything the Client Buys

Although it is sort of like an owner's manual, a "maximizer manual" goes beyond mere ownership to really helping the client *maximize* the investment. Now when I use the word "manual," it may conjure up a big book full of stuff no one reads, or a hard-to-follow, folded-up set of instructions in fourteen different languages. Although you can get as elaborate as you'd like, I'm generally talking about a very simple one-sheet overview with tips on how to MAXIMIZE whatever it is the client just purchased, as well as some post-buy steps we should set up.

Do you realize that most salespeople don't give their clients ANYTHING after the sale to help them maximize their investment? Nothing.

Now I'm not talking about *information* about the product (books, brochures, installation guides, etc.)—we usually have plenty of that. And I'm not talking about some helpful verbal tips we may share with the client right before he buys, or as he's taking ownership of the product ("Now make sure you do this . . ." or "Remember, don't let this or that happen . . ."). I'm talking about materials and meetings the client could use and/or attend to maximize their investment. These materials and meetings must be created *from the client's perspective, not ours.*

To go back to my radio example, instead of giving the

client nothing but a hearty handshake and an invoice, I could develop a simple one-sheet full of bullet points on how to maximize their radio schedule with our station—all written from the client's perspective. Which means I'm going to give the client not only tips on creating a better ad (no one does that step), but also some tips on how to best maximize the potential clients who may come in the door (and no one has certainly done that step).

This manual can also be delivered with a special gift, a way of saying "welcome to the family." Make the first time buy a big thing, especially if you'd like to form a long-term relationship with this client.

Step 2: Develop Post-Sale Check-Up Meetings

Once the sale is completed and clients begin to use your product or service, or are experiencing the benefits of implementing your product or service, they are going to be anxious to see the results. They may also have challenges and problems when using the product, for no matter how simple we feel something is, clients don't always follow all the steps or even open up the owner's manual. So it's important to have scheduled "check-ups" after the date of purchase or closing.

These meetings can be as formal or informal as you feel is necessary, and can take place either face-to-face or over the phone. You can also develop several follow-up check-lists and surveys to help solicit the type of feedback you need.

Even when you sell a service that is basically complete at the point of closing, such as the mortgage business, you can still come up with a post-closing check-up meeting, if for no other reason than to make sure the client was happy with the process and to get feedback on ways you could improve.

These types of meetings are excellent opportunities for up-selling clients into additional products or services (if they need them), or for getting referrals.

For some reason, even though past clients are five times more likely to buy than new clients and will provide referrals that are much easier to approach and turn into new customers, we have a block about contacting people after they buy.

An example I like to cite when talking with groups of business owners (who are as guilty of this as anybody) is a small landscaping company I had hired years ago to do a few outdoor projects at our home in Colorado. The project, which involved moving some dirt around and creating a small flagstone barbecue area, was just one of several we were "thinking" about doing.

The project proceeded on schedule and tuned out great, but that was it: Once it was done, it was done. In the landscaper's mind, what would he possibly need to discuss with us after his workers finished and packed up? Unless, of course, we have a problem, then he said to give him a call (which is what 90 percent of the companies consider post-buy service). So he only wanted to hear from me if we had a problem.

What about the rest of our projects we may want to get started over the coming months and years? What about all the referrals we'll have when people come to our home and see our new backyard barbecue area?

I don't know about you, but after about two or three weeks, I forgot the company's name that did the project, and certainly couldn't access their phone number.

Imagine if the landscaper had a few post-buy follow-up meeting? It would be so simple to set up, and could sound like this: "Mr. and Ms. Bennett, what I do that's different from other companies is schedule a few follow-up steps, and one of them is a personal visit in about three months. We survey the project to make sure everything is 100 percent, and we also apply an additional protective coat of finish on the exposed wood areas near the barbecue." Of course, when he shows up and looks at the project, it's the perfect time to discuss additional projects with us and maybe even collect the names of referrals.

Not only are these post-sale steps effective for providing service after the sale, they should be talked about early on, in the pre-sale stages, to help in the closing. We cover this in detail in the next step.

Step 3: Create Mini-Steps Out of Post-Buy Events and Use Them to Close the Sale

All of these follow-up tools and meetings need to be listed on your time-line as Mini-Steps, and they need to be talked about *before the sale* to help with closing. This sends a clear signal to the client that you're not going to run away, and that in fact the "partnership" is actually just beginning.

So with whatever post-buy things you develop, you'll need to break them out into tangible action-oriented Mini-Steps and treat them like you do the pre-buy steps: define deliverables, assign responsibility, pick rough delivery dates, and so forth.

These are particularly important indicators on your chances for closing the deal. If the client takes action on a post-buy Mini-Step, it's a strong indicator you're at a YES. If the client won't take action, it's a strong indicator that you're at a NO.

Here is how closing on a post-buy Mini-Step sounds:

> SALESPERSON: "Okay. Well, Mr. Client, with a potential closing date of March 31, we would tentatively (softener) do the orientation training for your people mid-April, starting around the 15th. We need to pencil in how many people could potentially (softener) be in that *training*.

The Bottom Line Is That No One Is Doing This!!

•   I buy a radio schedule. I *should receive* some tips on how to create an ad that really works, how to capture names when they call, how to price products, and how to package items together.

> What do I get now from 99 percent of all radio sellers? NOTHING.

•   I buy a piece of office furniture. I *should receive* some tips on how to create a more spacious, comfortable office, discounts on accessories, and so forth.

> What do I get now from 99 percent of all office furniture salespeople? NOTHING.

Just ask yourself this question:

"What would I do if I bought my own product or service to make sure it worked at a maximized level after I purchased it?"

Take those same steps and put together tools, information, meetings, personal involvement to help the client do the same thing.

HOW THIS POST-BUY PROCESS WORKS WITH RENEWAL TYPES OF PRODUCTS AND SERVICES

If you have a renewable type of product or service, where you lock people down over a series of weeks, months, or years, you should apply these same concepts to create a maximization process that accomplishes several objectives:

- You ensure they're maximizing their initial buy

- You keep the circling sharks away (the competition that comes swimming around when they sense there's some business someone's dug up)

- You take the client's temperature on a regular basis to head off small fever spikes before they turn into deadly infections

- You lock clients into a perpetual business relationship that will only expand and lead to an ongoing stream of referrals

It never ceases to amaze me how even consultative salespeople take the long-term relationship of a client for granted. We think just because we sold the deal, the renewal will take care of itself. So after the sale is completed (and we've got OUR needs met), we let the client take ownership, where chances are pretty good they'll not take the time or get the guidance to properly execute and maximize their investment. Or they'll have problems, and there won't be anyone to tell. If they DO hear from a salesperson it will be a casual, "Hey, how's it going?" The client, not wanting to cause conflict and acting from a trigger response, will say, "Pretty good," but meanwhile, inside they're steaming.

Or the seller will turn over the account to a customer service rep who is there should the client have problems. Of course studies have shown that when people have problems the vast majority (70 to 80 percent) tell no one at the company. They just decide (internally) to cancel, or to not renew, at the first opportunity.

The situation gets worse when renewal time comes around, and guess who magically shows up again carrying flowers and candy? You got it—the seller is back! Why? That's right, there is something in it for the seller!!!

Though we all would like to think we aren't quite that obvious, if you look at the post-buy steps we take and the way we act AFTER the client buys, I would imagine we'd see that we're probably doing something very similar. This certainly isn't what I'd call "consultative selling" or customer-centered selling at all!

We need to end this cycle, and as promised, I've got some simple steps for you to follow to make it happen:

- Identify client "touch points." These are purposeful points of contact you need to make with the client between selling cycles, whether it's over a two-week period or over a year. Touch points can be any number of contact methods—personal meetings, phone calls, e-mails, gifts, or social occasions.

- Just like you did with the Mini-Steps, get to a long table and lay down two points: Point 1 is when the initial sale took place, and Point 2 is when the renewal (next sale) takes place. Then get index cards and write the touch points on the cards, laying out the cards on the line between Points 1 and 2.

- Come up with some objectives for the touch points, such as what you are going to review in your quarterly "check-ups."

• To help with Consultative Closing, write these steps down and turn them into a presentation document you can share with clients, especially when selling new clients. It will greatly reduce the fear of failure on the part of new client, improve their ability to see a tangible R.O.I., and totally separate you from the competition. Here's how it might sound:

> SALESPERSON: "Lori, I know you're a bit nervous, having never done an annual program before. That's understandable . . . you're concerned about it working and making sure someone is there to help. Well, that's why we've designed a full Implementation and Maximization Program. As you can see here (showing the program) I will be meeting with your sales team at least four times a year, where we'll review the program objectives, analyze results, and make any tweaks we feel are necessary. I'm also going to invite you to these two client summits where you can sit with other clients and learn new ideas, network, and so on.

This next story is a lead-in to our final case study with the Denver Nuggets of the National Basketball Association. Since about 1991, I have consulted with over a hundred professional sports franchises in just about every major and minor league, including over forty NBA and NHL teams. I help them with their sales efforts in selling season tickets, groups, luxury suites, and advertising.

I can tell you after working closely with so many teams, only a very few had any sort of After-the-Sale sort of process in place. Ninety-nine percent of these teams (just like 99 percent of all businesses) did NOTHING for the customer after they bought. When I say "nothing," I don't mean they ignored them completely. They provided a good product on the floor, field, or ice, and they had good customer service folks who were available and would make occasional contact. But as far as an owner's manual for maximizing what the customer just bought (the season tickets, the suite, etc.) the teams provided NO GUIDANCE.

Clients would think: "Great, so I just dropped $150,000 on a suite for basketball and hockey, and no one has given me even a tip sheet on how to use the thing. Everyone just expects that I know what I'm doing. Well, I don't!!"

So what would happen is that clients would take ownership of their tickets or suite or ad in the game program, without knowing how to maximize the investment. Thus, they'd make major mistakes. For instance, in the area of season tickets, clients were getting the tickets at the beginning of the year and shoving them in a drawer. Then suddenly there'd be a game and they'd run around trying to get people to go, or they'd completely miss a game and the seats would go unused. So at the end of the year, the salespeople would show up and want to renew the client and they'd be greeted with, "I've got a damn drawer full of tickets from last year. I don't want to do it again."

Well, the problem was, no one bothered to show the client how to properly use those tickets strategically by planning the entire year, and pushing them out into the hands of salespeople and clients.

Raising Their Game by Focusing on What Happens *After* the Client Buys

The Denver Nuggets were my first client inside pro sports, starting back in 1991. At that time, Paul Andrews, whom I interviewed for this case study, was in an account executive position; since then, he's risen through the ranks and is now the executive vice president/chief marketing officer for Kroenke Sports Enterprises, owners of the Nuggets as well as the Colorado Avalanche of the National Hockey League, and several other sports and entertainment entities. According to Paul Andrews:

"We're talking about a team (the Nuggets) that for nine years in a row didn't make the playoffs and had the worst record in the league for two of those years. And still, because of our maximization program and focus on after the sale, 75 to 80 percent of those clients renewed, even in the toughest year. It was all due to the partnership mindset, because team-performance-wise we were terrible. On the other side of the spectrum we had the Avalanche, one of the best teams in the league ever since they arrived in Denver. On the partnering side with the Avalanche, our goal was to steadily improve renewals, and we were able to take renewals from 92 or 93 percent to 97 or 98 percent, and that delta represents millions of dollars to us. Whatever the team situation—good or bad for the moment—clients have to feel there is someone they can talk to, someone who has partnered with them to create a customized plan.

"A great example would be a Mexican restaurant we saw a few years back. Their biggest problem was they couldn't get anyone to come to their restaurant in December. Originally, when we first sat down with them, they had no interest in buying season tickets. But then we went through our needs analysis, and gave them a customized recommendation that included several creative ideas for after they owned the tickets, like doing a 'fish-bowl drawing' using our tickets as the draw in September and November: Basically it's people who drop their card or name in the fishbowl would get tickets. In our follow-up meetings we found that the program was working great to create a database they could market out to in December, offering a free appetizer to anyone who came back in that month. The results were phenomenal. And this was with business owners who didn't like basketball, frankly, but they knew they could use those tickets to attract customers and get people in the restaurant in the slow months. That's effective partnering.

"If you want to build a solid relationship that will last, you need to give them ideas that will make them money, and give them a plan or maximization guide to follow after the sale. Plus, those check-in meetings we did turned into a great opportunity to sell additional inventory items the client may have a need for."

According to Andrews, the elements of the Nuggets and Avalanche Maximization Program are:

- A gift and note from top management is sent with the delivery of the tickets, saying "Welcome to the Family."
- Several follow-up visits are planned during the year.
- Clients are given a ticket maximization program to help manage the inventory.
- The team offers a reward program where clients can earn gifts for effectively using their tickets.

SOME FREQUENTLY ASKED QUESTIONS ON CLOSING BY FOCUSING ON THE AFTER THE SALE

Q: *I'm still unclear on how to close now, before the sale, using something that happens after the sale. Can you give some examples?*

A: Sure, and I can understand why it's a bit confusing. We're just not used to doing it since we're so focused on the BEFORE the sale process, and our own bells, whistles, and needs. The thing to keep in mind is that even though we're talking with a client BEFORE he buys, he's already thinking of life AFTER the potential sale: "If I buy this, how will it make me feel? What will others think about me? Will it keep me from buying other things? Will I have to hassle with it all the time?"

So it's not like it's going to be a stretch to get the client to tell us what he's thinking and feeling about a possible life after he owns our product or service: The movie (good or bad) is already playing.

The way we practice consultative closing with "After the Sale" is to start scheduling in the post-buy Mini-Steps we have in our new defined process. These are just like Mini-Steps elsewhere: If clients take action, or they don't take action, they'll be "telling" us where they truly are in the decision-making process.

Here are two examples:

1. "Kaitlin, these classes fill up. We need to get you tentatively scheduled in the free training course on that camera."

2. "Ryan, should we move forward? I need to know the various departments we'd want to invite to the

initial product launch kick-off and celebration, so we'd like to give our caterer a heads-up of how many to expect."

Here is an extra note: I like to introduce a third party into the equation in the After-the-Sale process, like the caterer listed in the example above. This transfers some of the pressure of the close to an outside entity instead of always having it come from me.

Q: *How elaborate should our "owner's manual" be and how much do you recommend putting in there?*

A: I'd say make it consistent with the price level and level of complexity of your product or service. That means if your product costs $30 or $40 and it's easy to grasp and understand, you probably don't need to produce a leather-bound owner's guide with tons of tips and ideas on maximizing the investment. For a product of that size you can still provide a one-sheeter with several bullet points.

And if you're product is expensive, has several levels of complexity, and can be easily MIS-used, then I'd say you should have a fairly elaborate follow-up process: not just the manual, but have meetings, classes, and workshops as well.

Just remember that the "owner's manual" isn't designed to just cover the basics of how to use the product. It needs to contain some strategy on how to maximize the product or service. Big difference! An owner's manual for a new suit could just cover the suit and how to store it, or it could give me several strategies for maximizing my new suit, tips on when to wear what and why, how to match it with different accessories, and so on. *Wouldn't that be a cool thing to have?*

These are all simple, very simple things we can sit

down and knock out in an afternoon. And the beauty is that you'll run circles around your competition because they WON'T EVEN HAVE a manual of any kind.

Q: *What if there is normally little follow-up or service after the sale? Can you still use that for pre-buy closing?*

A: Sure, but you may have to create some things you normally wouldn't (which will only further separate you from the competition). Even if you have the type of product or service where you probably wouldn't "partner" with a client to maximize their investment (for instance, you're selling high-end women's shoes), you can still add value by looking at the TYPE OF PERSON who buys and not necessarily at the product itself. So even though you're not going to get together again with the client to see how the shoes are working, you can still invite the client to a special workshop on "dressing for success" that your company cosponsors or puts on.

When you have something like this you can say, "While you're thinking about which shoes you'd like, I want to mention that we have a special workshop we're holding for all clients who've purchased over $100 with us over the past 90 days. It's a great program on "Dressing Tips for Successful Business Women," and it's supposed to be very good. You can also bring a guest. If you were (softener) to go, who would you most likely invite? I'll at least pencil you in."

Q: *What if you give a client all the follow-up materials and meetings and they don't take advantage of any of it?*

A: Well, you certainly can't force people to read the instruction manual on a product, but it's still the right thing to do, to at least provide it. Remember, this is a partnership, and all you can do is be the best partner you can be in the relationship. You'll still get a great deal of credit, even if the client doesn't follow your tips and suggestions. This is particularly helpful when things go wrong. Clients will be able to share in the blame if they didn't follow your guide. (That's not to say it's a good thing, but at least they can't blame you 100 percent when you didn't really do anything.)

REVIEW

• Consultative selling is supposed to be all about merging the two sides of the sales equation (the before the sale and after the sale, as well as the roles of salesperson on one side and client on the other) into one seamless process.

• Most salespeople, even consultative salespeople, are terrible AFTER the sale is executed and the clients "take ownership."

• We must help clients not only to use our product or service, but to maximize their investment. This includes creating an "owner's manual" for every piece of inventory we sell.

• For longer-term engagements with renewals, we need to establish critical "touch points," where we'll check in and take the client's temperature throughout the engagement.

Bonus Materials Available at the Online Resource Center:

• Written examples of "owner's manuals" from real clients.

CHAPTER 7

Consultative Closing for Managers (a Short Course)

I have worked with many sales organizations over the years, and unfortunately too many of those organizations look at training and skill-set improvement as something that starts and stops at the salesperson level. They send their salespeople off to "get fixed," only to bring them right back into a dysfunctional system, run by managers who aren't maximizing the new skills of the sellers, or aren't developing the critical tools and disciplines required to achieve success with my methodology.

In order to become a truly effective Consultative Closing organization, everyone must be on the same page and operating in a structure that reinforces the critical elements of the system. In this chapter I'm going to outline some of those critical elements as they pertain to sales management and top management, and show you how you can start to implement these concepts in order to achieve maximum performance and accountability.

Management plays a critical role in holding salespeople accountable for doing more of the right things, particularly consultative salespeople who by their nature have a tendency to err on the side of being nice, friendly, and letting things linger way too long in their pipeline.

One overriding theme I have when working with managers is that *salespeople will hold clients accountable to the exact degree that the manager holds them accountable.*

> If a salesperson comes back from a sales call and the manager does nothing more than ask a few quick, surface-level questions, like, "So . . . how'd it go?"
>
> And if the seller responds with, "Yeah, I think it went pretty well. The guy seemed real interested."
>
> And if that manager stops there with a quick high-five saying, "You rock!"
>
> Then the seller soon learns that that is all he needs to get from the client.

If, however, the sales manager starts to probe and ask more detailed questions like, "What does 'went pretty well' mean?" and "When you say 'interested' what does it mean?" the seller will soon realize that, "If I'm going to be asked these types of questions when I get back, I might as well ask the client."

Managers play a critical role in the effective implementation of any new training concepts and ideas, especially many of the ideas I teach, for they have to do as much with the changing of the entire system and procedures as they do with simply changing what a salesperson says. Managers set the bar, establish the performance standards, and must take the lead in creating lasting change.

MANAGEMENT AND MINI-STEPS

Management must take the lead in developing the Mini-Steps within the sales process. Of course, salespeople should participate, since they're the ones most consistently on the front lines, and buy-in is always important for total ownership. But management needs to be involved in order to drive the initiative down through the organization.

Managers should use the experience of creating the Mini-Steps as a productive group-learning experience. When everyone is together in the same room, working on the steps, and laying them out on the table, it can not only communicate the information, but make a strong point about how everyone is working from the same play book:

- Get in a room with a long conference table.

- Get out the 3×5 cards, color-code them if you'd like, and write the Mini-Steps on the cards.

- Establish a sample Closing Date, then lay out the cards for before the sale and after the sale.

- Make sure everyone knows roughly when the steps should happen and who is responsible for taking the action. Be sure to remind salespeople that some of the steps can happen simultaneously, and very quickly if the client is ready to move.

- Also note the most important steps, and which ones should be shared with the client.

Once everything is laid out, go over the steps and determine the percentage chance at each stage. For instance, "deliver initial proposal—25 percent," which means that if we get the client to take this step, 25 percent of the time they end up closing for a YES. This is an important step because we're so used to having twenty different interpretations of what "90 percent" means: Seller 1 thinks it means this, seller 2 thinks it means that, while the manager thinks

it means something completely different. By attaching percentages to every step, we take away the dangerous inter-
preting, and we put the task actually in the hands of the
client, and the action or inaction on a Mini-Step. The idea
is to remove the verbal spin and the dangerous 40 percent
gap we covered earlier.

The goal for management should be to eventually get
to a place where the manager can tell the salesperson where
his pipeline is, based on what prospects have actually done
versus a verbal interpretation of where the salesperson feels
the prospect may be. This will make a huge difference in
forecasting and planning.

Another really powerful reason to have a Mini-Step
process in place is to get rid of what I call "metal pipelines," or pipelines managers can't see into. Right now
many managers manage only outcomes: running around
collecting whatever comes out of the bottom of the sales
funnels—funnels they can't see into. Of course, by the time
the outcome comes out, it's usually too late to affect the
performance. In other words, if managers are only managing outcomes, and the outcome they get from seller X turns
out to be 50 percent of what she needs, and there are only
three days left in the month, then it's probably too late to
do much to save her.

Instead, we want to build "clear pipelines," where management can see into the inner workings of what is going
on, where opportunities truly are, when there is still time to
do something about a slow month from seller X. Mini-Steps
enable managers to do this much more effectively, because
there are tangible action-steps attached to advancing
through the pipeline, and not just the verbal dreams of
salespeople. So if a salesperson says, "Hey, boss, I'd say the
Bennetts are at 90 percent on going with our windows," the
manager can say, "Well, let's see what the Bennetts' activity

is telling us. It looks like they haven't taken anything beyond step 5, and as you know, no one is at 90 percent unless they've done everything up to step 9. So really, were are they?" The salesperson now has a clear path to take with the Bennetts: Get them from step 5 to step 9.

When there are clear pipelines, the manager can see where opportunities are and know where to hop in and help. Instead of just saying to the seller, "Well, see if you can call the Bennetts and ask where they are . . ." the manager can say, "Why don't you call the Bennetts and ask them to commit to the engineering analysis?" Also, with Mini-Steps the manager can see that the seller may have the Bennetts between steps 5 and 6, and it would make sense to hop in and help at that particular stage.

Managers should want to step in and help on the front lines, at critical points in the process, but if all you have is a vague two-step system and metal pipelines, it's really tough to guess when and where to hop in.

MANAGEMENT AND EMBRACING NO

Going to NO is also an unnatural place for sales managers, not just for salespeople. This means that managers, who are the main work influence for salespeople, will play a critical role in teaching and encouraging salespeople to embrace NO as a possible outcome. One of the main reasons salespeople come back from calls and tell overly positive stories is they want to impress the sales manager and show that they know what they're doing: "Yeah, I'm good boss, I know what I'm doing. No one would ever say NO to me, or lie to me. I'm telling you, this deal is going to be big . . . VERY big."

And it's easy to see how managers can get caught up in the enthusiasm and positive energy. They like to be liked and accepted and not seen as a pessimist: "Great job, buddy. So you think it could really turn into something? Sweet. You da man." (High fives all around.)

Plus, managers also like to have good stories to tell *their* bosses in top management. Embracing NO needs to start at the very top, where upper management is communicating the new mantra: *We Value Reality . . . Not Spin. (*Or maybe: *"Spin Kills."*)

- Closing is YES or NO

- NO is better than MAYBE: Better for the client, better for the salesperson, better for the organization

- NO is not a death sentence, but in many cases it's what must happen on the way to YES

Soon top management will start asking tougher questions of local managers, who will do the same with salespeople, who will eventually ask clients for reality and not spin. And when the entire system is embracing NO and focusing on concrete action steps versus verbal confirmation, then the culture has been changed.

While it is a company-wide, top-down, cultural shift that needs to take place, the day-to-day responsibility of making the whole thing work really falls on the local sales manager. The local sales manager is the driving force in the middle of the process—with salespeople "below" him, and upper management "above" him. He must learn to embrace NO and demand reality on a daily basis in dealing with salespeople and clients, and then communicate what is real to upper management.

Here are some steps managers can take to start embracing NO:

• Clearly communicate to the entire sales team that a new level of accountability and reporting is being put into place FOR EVERYONE: not just for salespeople (it's nothing personal), but for management and the organization as a whole. The reasons are:

> *It's better for the client . . . better for salespeople . . . better for business.*

• Explain to the sales team that on occasion there will be a more thorough "debriefing" after a sales call (not after every call, but maybe one or two a week with each salesperson, depending on how many people are on a team), and that the manager will be holding the salesperson accountable for the same type of realistic answers the salespeople should be holding clients accountable for:

> For example, the response, "They're interested," will be challenged with, "Great, what does that mean?" rather than, "Great . . . put it on the board."

> The whole idea is not to be a hardass, but to drive reality throughout the organization.

• When doing a call debriefing with a salesperson you can still be friendly and positive, but be direct and unwilling to accept spin. This is tough love: Salespeople will grow from the experience and become better for it. And the same level of questioning must be applied to every salesperson, it can't be a random thing doled out to just a few.

•   When a salesperson *does* come back with a NO
from a client, don't immediately start attacking with things
they need to do to get back in there and turn it around. You
need to first listen, then give the seller positive affirmation
for getting a decision (remember we said YES or NO).
THEN start talking about the issues they discovered in NO,
and the action plan in moving forward—in other words, is it
NO-FOR-NOW, or NO-FOR-EVER? Communicate that the
seller is never going to get to YES until they've gone
through NO, so where they are is one step closer to doing
the deal.

It can be all be boiled down to this: Once salespeople
understand that they're going to be made fun of much more
around the office by coming back and reporting the client
is "interested . . . VERY interested" as opposed to saying
that "He's at a NO for now and there are three things to
address"—life will be changing for the positive.

A SAMPLE CALL DEBRIEFING

I've coached hundreds of sales managers on how to effectively do a debriefing after a call. Here is a sample of what
the interaction sounds like:

> SALES MANAGER: "So tell me about today's call, Bob. I
> know you were going out there to ABC with the
> purpose of getting him to take action on a few
> Mini-Steps, right?"

> SALESPERSON: "Yes, because he is scheduled to start
> soon I wanted to get names in seats for the
> installation training and an implementation
> schedule."

SALES MANAGER: "Sounds about right for where they are. So tell me about the call. And again, we're after the reality of what actually happened, not just your interpretation of what you THINK may have happened, right?" (teaching moment)

SALESPERSON: "Oh yeah, I know what you mean. Okay, let me start. Basically the call went great from the start. . . ."

SALES MANAGER: "Good, good. Did you set the agenda at the beginning of the call and tell him we were going to ask for a decision at the end?"

SALESPERSON: "Uh, yeah. Well, I think . . . well, I guess not. Not a very good one anyway."

SALES MANAGER: "Okay. Just remember we should always start with a good agenda, especially when we're asking for Mini-Step action. And it's easy to skip over it if we're not careful, we all do it, so just be aware. Okay, continue. . . ." (teaching moment)

SALESPERSON: "I have to remember that. Okay. Well, we talked back and forth and eventually I told him that we needed to get names in seats and an implementation schedule, and he seemed fine with everything. . . ." (commencing the spin)

SALES MANAGER: "Now when you say, "seemed fine," are you saying he gave you the names and you got the schedule?" (tough love teaching moment)

SALESPERSON: "Well, he said he couldn't do it right then because he still needed to talk to a few other people in the process, but he said everything still looked good."

SALES MANAGER: "What does "looked good" mean?" (teaching moment)

SALESPERSON:"Well, he said as far as he knew the project was still a go. He just had to talk to a few other departments before he could give us names for who was going to be in the seats."

SALES MANAGER: "But these names are just tentative, and the implementation schedule isn't binding. Sounds like there might be some issues hiding beneath the surface here?"

SALESPERSON: "No, no. I don't think so (now in full spin cycle). I think he wants to work with us."

SALES MANAGER: "Bob, I know you've worked hard on this for some time now, and it's a major part of your hitting your fourth quarter objectives. But it's apparent, based on what the client is actually doing—or not doing—and not just what he's saying, that this opportunity is not as close as you're thinking." (I know you've got a major crush on her, but she doesn't love you, dude.)

SALESPERSON: "Well, I'm not ready to say that. I mean, he's given me nothing but green light signals every step of the way."

SALES MANAGER: "Yes, I know what you're saying. Let's do this. Let me give him a quick call with you right here and let me play the heavy. I'll just ask him from a planning standpoint where we are, and I won't attack or anything like that, okay?"

SALESPERSON: "Sure, can't hurt at this point."

SALES MANAGER (dials a phone number, client picks
up): "Tom, it's Roger Porter, Bob Yantis's manager over at XYZ. How are you? Good, good.
Hey, I've got Bob in here with me and he was
just telling me a bit about his visit out there with
you today. Yeah, yeah, he is a great guy, for
sure. Anyway, I was just trying to do some resource allocation planning for the fourth quarter and into next year, and he said you all were
excited about working with us, but not quite
ready to commit to an implementation plan.
And that concerned me a bit because I know
what our staffing issue is going to look like with
the new product launch we're rolling out in November. Of course, Bob couldn't know that, so
I thought I'd call and get your take. Is this really
going to happen in the fourth quarter? (Pause
. . . Manager shakes his head NO at the salesperson.) So we're probably closer to a NO at this
point than a YES, right? Okay, well let me ask
you this . . . (Now he starts taking the client all
the way into NO to discover reasons and see if
there are issues to be dealt with on the way back
to a possible YES.)

Embracing NO is tough love. The salesperson may
freak out at the thought of losing the client, but the manager knows that he must go into the Ugly Pond and fish
out the issues that lie beneath the surface, which must be
addressed before moving back to YES. The salesperson
needs to understand his own tendency to want (*and desperately need*) to hear certain answers (he can only afford to

hear and pretend YES or MAYBE), and the client's tendency to dole out those falsely positive answers in order to avoid conflict.

The key, of course, to embracing NO is knowing how to follow through with the process and how to bring a number of NO clients back to YES, knowing that NO is not a life sentence, but that MAYBE *is* the killer.

MANAGEMENT AND FOCUSING ON AFTER THE SALE

Many managers are already involved in the post-buy process because they get called on to solve any issues or problems with delivery: They are the ones who have to put out the fires. And while that service is important and probably won't change, what I'm talking about is a more active role in the post-buy process on the positive side, one where the manager is actively engaged with the client to help him maximize his investment instead of just sitting and waiting for problems to pop up.

The question then becomes, What should a manager do after the sale to effect a positive outcome? Here are a few ideas:

• Make the client feel special to the whole company, not just the salesperson, by:

1. Writing a letter to every client after a buy. This can be an automated form letter, but it will have more impact if you take the time to hand-write a short note.

2. Sending a gift from the manager (aka the company). Again, this can be a generic gift with an attached note, but the more personal the better.

• Make the client feel like she has just joined an entire family of caring people who desperately want her to succeed:

1. Does the manager know WHY the client is buying, or just the size of the package she bought? Most managers know just the details from the company's side: what was purchased, but not what the client was hoping to accomplish. Encourage salespeople to take good notes so that as manager you can go through the needs analysis and get a good understanding of what the client hopes will happen after she buys.

2. A simple thing like a personal visit, phone call, or e-mail after the initial buy is a big deal to most clients. Everyone wants to feel that their purchase meant something special inside the company.

Another important reason managers should care about forming a client relationship after the sale has to do with strengthening the bond between the client and the company, and not just allowing the relationship to exist between the client and the salesperson. Salespeople leave. They go to the competition, and usually they walk out the door with their customer list or Rolodex file. A company can be severely hurt if there is no relationship between the client and management and top management.

MANAGEMENT AND PROSPECTING: MAINTAINING HEALTHY PIPELINES

This is an area I typically have to invest a good deal of time in when consulting with a client, mainly because managers are so focused on the outcome and not on the process involved in creating that outcome. And because they aren't watching how efficiently the pipeline is working, they're unable to provide much helpful guidance when it comes to prospecting activities of their people. Sure they can run around, spouting the need to "pick it up, folks," and "get on the phone and make some calls," but can they really provide meaningful feedback on an individual basis as to what each salesperson should be doing on a daily basis?

Unfortunately, most managers don't know what the prospecting level should be in order to create enough cool, warm, and hot leads. All of this has a direct impact on the salesperson's closing effectiveness, for if they don't have enough irons in the fire, they're going to be weak closers, mainly because they can't afford to take people to NO.

Some Simple Steps for Managers to Improve Prospecting Accountability

• Establish a solid average number of new business calls each person on the team must make on a weekly basis in order to adequately fill the pipeline on a regular basis.

• When the salesperson gets busy, establish a minimum number of new calls each salesperson must make, even in their busiest times.

• Introduce staff-wide mandatory prospecting times. This one step has had a more positive impact on the overall prospecting effectiveness of my clients than anything else I have suggested. Whether you decide to do it once, twice, or three times a week, the fact that everyone in the office—and perhaps across the entire company—is involved in new business efforts sends a strong signal to each person on the staff. It also provides a great support system for salespeople who otherwise may quit after a few calls on their own.

•   Pay particular attention to salespeople who have a lot of pending business in their pipeline, because their tendency will be to stop for a while to "catch up." We all have a desire to do the safer, seemingly more productive thing, rather than pick up the phone and make new contacts.

REVIEW

• Salespeople will hold clients accountable to the exact degree that the manager holds them accountable.

• Management must take the lead in developing the Mini-Steps within the sales process.

• Instead of salespeople guessing as to the closing percentage with opportunities in the pipeline, managers can see where opportunities truly are based on the client taking action or not taking action (which are attached to a percentage chance of a YES close).

• Managers have to be the strongest advocate of Embracing NO as a culture. They need to reject a false "maybe" from the salesperson, and help them move toward NO.

• Managers must do a more realistic and thorough call debriefing after a sales call, asking pointed questions of sellers and insisting on YES or NO answers.

• Managers should be particularly interested in developing the post-buy process because it's critical for management and the company to form a relationship with the client, and not let it reside totally with the salesperson (who can leave at any time and walk out the door with all the client relationships).

Bonus Materials Available at the Online Resource Center:

• A video streamed role play with me as sales manager doing a call debriefing with a salesperson. (MP3 audio and a written transcript are available as well.)

CHAPTER 8

A Four-Week Plan
for Implementation
and Lasting Success

Like all new training information, including what I present in my live workshops and seminars, information becomes real only when it is put it into action in the real world. The next thirty days are critical for putting the ideas and concepts put forth in this book into action, so that they become a part of your long-term strategy for success. I have made several additional tools available for you because I feel that we are partners in our long-term success. If I can help you maximize your investment in my book, you will be more likely to tell others, and be open to buying future books. I win only if you win . . . and that's the way all sales should be.

With that in mind I've come up with a four-week plan for not only implementing the concepts and ideas included in the book, but for hopefully making them a permanent part of what you do. We all know that doing what's good for us for just a short time, without changing our long-term behavior, only leads to temporary results.

If you've already done some of the steps while reading the book, just check them off as completed and keep going:

WEEK 1

❑ *Developing Mini-Steps*

- Get 3×5 cards and write each Mini-Step you currently have, along with ones you need to create, on a card. If you want to take an extra step and get colored cards, or get some colored stickers to signify different types of steps, that can be even more effective.

- Establish a representative Closing Date, and lay that out width-wise across a table, using a piece of tape, string, etc.

- Now begin to lay out the 3×5 cards on a timeline before, during, and after the closing date.

- Once the cards are all laid out, go back and see whether there are steps you need to add, subtract, or change.

- Mark or use your color-code system to indicate which steps you're going to share with the client during the sales process.

- Look through the various steps in the process and mark significant steps that signify progress towards a successful close, and assign an estimated percentage to the step. For example, you may have a step named "Final Proposal," and because 75 percent of what gets to the final proposal stage ends up closing for a YES, mark that step: "75 percent."

- Once completed, develop a basic document that lays out your Mini-Step process, and indicate which steps are to be shared with clients, and the estimated closing percentage on those steps deemed critical.

❑ *Embracing NO as a Culture*

- Make a list of all the opportunities you now have in the pipeline.

- Next to each opportunity that is not at a YES (with appropriate action steps), mark NO-FOR-NOW, and then list the concrete reasons it's at NO. If you don't know, or aren't sure (it does no good to guess), call those prospects and ask: "Out of curiosity (softener), why exactly have we not moved forward with at least (mention a Mini-Step)?"

- Listen to the response and determine whether the client should move forward toward another step. If it is really a NO, get it out of the pipeline.

❑ *Focusing on After the Sale*

- In conjunction with your post-buy Mini-Steps review, list what you give clients to help them not only to use your product, but to maximize their investment. Think of yourself owning the product or service. Knowing what you know, what would you do to make sure you get the most from your product?

- If you have several different products or levels of service, make a checklist of things a client should do for each one.

❑ *Extra Tips*

- Even though these are important steps for you to take, don't neglect other less comfortable tasks you should be doing as well, such as business development or working on closing a tough customer.

- Schedule time to go online and review some of the support materials I offer. Also review different elements of the book you found helpful. Make sure the concepts remain fresh in your mind and don't slip away.

WEEK 2

❑ *Developing Mini-Steps*

- Make your Mini-Steps accessible wherever you have client contact—in your office, cubicle, or in your notebook—and even write the steps on a card you can easily carry with you. The idea is to keep the next steps in mind as you go through the closing process with the client.

- Work on developing action-oriented questions using the Mini-Steps you've identified. Review the information on creating the Assumptive Request questions from Chapter 4, and insert your Mini-Steps.

❑ *Embracing NO as a Culture*

- If you have a sales manager, or are a sales manager, review the debriefing process after a call to make sure you're asking clear questions that get a firm response.

❑   *Focusing on After the Sale*

- If you have a renewable product or service, you need to establish strategic touch points in between renewal time periods. If it's an annual cycle, the touch points may happen on a quarterly basis, or more or less often, depending on your particular situation.

- Record these touch points, and describe the activities that should take place in each touch point meeting. For instance, these activities could be:
  —Review key initiatives
  —Chart established benchmarks

You'll want to show these steps to the client and talk about their implementation early on in the sales process.

❑   *Extra Tip*

- Now that you've no doubt had the opportunity to try a few of the concepts, you may be a little frustrated because things aren't working out exactly as described in the book. That's totally understandable and to be expected. Learning new strategies and concepts you'll adapt as your own takes time, persistence, and patience. Just because the concepts are "simple" to grasp doesn't mean they're easy to do. It's sort of like losing weight and getting in shape. The steps are simple—eat less, work out more—but doing it regularly can be very, very hard. Whenever you break old habits and change long-held belief systems you're going to be in for a fight. Hang in there, do a little more each day (even on the toughest days), and don't ever give up. If you need encouragement or help, please remember to plug into our online community, or e-mail me for help. That's what I'm here for.

WEEK 3

❏ *Developing Mini-Steps*

- Analyze the performance of your Mini-Steps and the action-oriented questions you're using in conjunction with them:

Are the steps easy to explain and easy to understand on the part of the client?

Do they make sense?

Are clients giving you answers that are backed by action, or no action?

Is the percentage-of-close attached to each step in line with reality?

❏ *Embracing NO as a Culture*

- Embracing NO takes continuous practice and self-checking to make sure you're not sliding back into old habits. The easiest way to test whether you're going to NO, or settling with MAYBE, is to only allow yourself only two options: YES or NO, with reasons.

- After each call, go to clients you've allowed to slip back into MAYBE and ask them for clarification on where they truly are:

Assume the client is at NO when you make the call ("Liz, you've had this proposal for a few weeks, I'm assuming you're at a NO for now . . .") It really is a no-lose situation. If the client agrees with you you'll get the truth and can change them or move on. If they argue with you, it means they'll be coming back toward the positive.

❑   *Focusing on After the Sale*

- Your focus this week should be on building and supporting an effective network, or a NET that WORKS, and it's going to feature your current and future clients. Do you have your clients on a program that enables easy contact, such as *Outlook* or another Customers Relationship Management tool?

- One way to support your network is to tell customers that your ongoing touch points are excellent opportunities to do some networking. And not just for your needs. Networking can also help the client solve a particular challenge (could be a challenge related to something other than your product).

❑   *Extra Tip*

- This week invest an hour or more immersed in a client's business, not selling them, but actually working in the business or just walking around and observing. Watch how they do what they do, see the challenges they face, and hear their struggles. Observe how they may be using, or not using, your product or service. Encourage them to be honest in their feedback. This one step, done maybe two or three times a year (perhaps more if your business model demands it) will help you see and hear reality, and will help you develop better long-term partnerships not only with that client, but with all future clients.

WEEK 4

❑   *Developing Mini-Steps*

•   Review your Mini-Step process from start to finish. Now that you've had a chance to use the various steps, you may want to lay the cards out again on the table. Consider changing around the order, or adding or subtracting a few steps.

•   As you track the progress of prospects in the pipeline, make sure whatever tool you're using for Customer Relationship Management (e.g., *Outlook* or *ACT*) is using the Mini-Steps you've established. It does no good to have all the steps in place if you can't look at your pipeline and see where opportunities are according to the action steps.

❑   *Embracing NO as a Culture*

•   Review the "Going to NO" questions in the book, as well as the many resources I make available online. Of all the skill sets contained in the book, this is the one area where you must be on constant guard against slipping back into bad habits. This happens because there is no one to catch you accepting MAYBE—it's just you and the client in the meeting. If she says MAYBE and you say "Good enough," who's going to know?

- Make it a habit to ask yourself after each client contact, "Did I get a YES for action?" If the answer is, "No, I didn't," or "I'm not sure," then you're being seduced back into Maybe-Land and you need to pick up the phone and clarify exactly what happened and where you are:

"Mike, I know I just saw you earlier today, but I got back to the office and realized I hadn't asked you whether you're going to send me the artwork or I should pick it up from the agency. Which one is it?"

❑ *Focusing on After the Sale*

- You need to review your total After-the-Sale program. Is it something that will truly help a client understand not only how to use the product, but more importantly, how to maximize their investment?

- Talk with a few clients about the program and ask them how they feel. For example:

Does this step make you feel like you're part of the family right away? If so, why? If not, why not? What should we add or take away?

How do you see the mid-buy touch points helping you? What other things should we be asking about?

❑ *Extra Tip*

- Schedule a time once a month (at least) for reviewing the core elements contained in this book. Even if you invest just an hour a month to look at your Mini-Steps, Embracing NO, and Selling After the Sale, you'll identify problem areas and keep the concepts fresh in your mind.

Seven Sample Mini-Step Processes from Different Types of Businesses

These generic steps are developed to show how Mini-Step Closing can be applied to any business category. Though I've consulted and trained with clients in nearly all these business categories, I don't pretend to know your business well enough to add the specific action steps you require. If you don't see your business category listed, look for a similar one to model your system after.

1. RADIO AND TV SALES

The way most radio and TV ad salespeople sell is to approach businesses and try and get them to invest in advertising schedules that can last anywhere from a few days to several weeks and months. The length of the sales cycle depends on how prepared and savvy about advertising the client is (e.g., do they have an ad already written, have they purchased time before). With new clients, the salesperson has to do a good deal of persuading as to why the client should go with her station over others, and then work with the client to develop a schedule and an ad to run. Timing is also a challenge, as clients may say, "I may go with your station, but not until fourth quarter," or "Our budget is spent for this year, but come see me next January and we'll take another look at it." (Of course, it's usually NOT a budget issue at all, but more of a return-on-investment issue.)

Here are some of the Mini-Steps I suggest:

Tangible "To-Do" Tasks (just a few to give you some ideas)

- Sign contract signed or agree to schedule

- Get schedule turned in

- Get deposit and/or credit application

Special Events to Which to Invite Clients Early On

- Can you create a "Welcome to the Station" breakfast, or lunch? Something just for first-time buyers as a way of saying, "Welcome to the Family"?

- How about a free seminar just for people who are considering radio or TV? This would be an informal breakfast you hold once a month with maybe twenty or thirty prospective clients, where you can go over the pros and cons, answer questions, and so forth.

Steps to Get the Client More Excited or Perhaps to Make Better Decisions

- Set up a brainstorming meeting with your creative group

- Set up a meeting at the client's office to address their people

- Set up a "cross promotion" analysis meeting
- Do a station tour to meet personalities or the announcer doing the ad

Steps to Secure Inventory, Production, or Delivery Times

- Set up inventory priority system for pre-booking time. Thus, when a client says he wants to go on the air in six months, he can put his name down and get a priority number. (This will start to separate the lookers from the buyers.)
- Set up a studio booking system by appointment only, or with certain announcers.

Steps to Help Fulfill the Order

- Schedule date of commercial production (perhaps the client would like to attend?)
- Send date and times of ads to client

Post-Buy Mini-Steps

- Send a special gift to first-time buyers (not a step you'd share with clients, more as an internal reminder)
- Hold mid-schedule analysis meeting (a meeting about midway through the initial ad schedule)
- Hold post-schedule analysis meeting and planning session

Note: Remember to pick a "Start Date" when planning.

2. SPORTS INVENTORY

Sports inventory can include season tickets, group tickets, etc.

Tangible "To-Do" Tasks (just a few to give you some ideas)

- Contract in

- Seats selected

- Initial deposit or full payment in

Special Events to Which to Invite Clients Early On

- Develop a "Meet the Coach" breakfast or lunch, exclusively for first time clients. Even if a client is months away from making a final decision, you can at least pencil in their name for the soon-to-be-sold-out lunch.

- Send out invitations to the suite to businesses that are contemplating investing in season tickets (or whatever inventory item you're selling), an "Introduction to Sports Marketing" type of event.

Steps to Get the Client More Excited or Perhaps to Make Better Decisions

- Invite the client and a select number of her people to come down for the seat selection process and maybe a special tour (combined with other groups to save time).

- Set up a date to drop the tickets off at the client, and if a big sale, bring the team mascot along, along with a big team banner. TAKE PICTURES. Make it a big deal.

- Invite clients to a big group meeting you schedule at the same time every month for business owners who are even contemplating buying sports inventory.

Steps to Secure Inventory, Production, or Delivery Times

- Develop a booking priority system (most teams already have them, but may not highlight them to clients) where clients put their name down on a list, saying they want this section, or these particular seats, or this particular sign in the arena.

- Offering refundable deposits is always good for securing early sales. Of course, you have to analyze how many you have to refund, but chances are good that once someone puts something down, they'll follow through.

Steps to Help Fulfill the Order

- Contract is signed and turned in.

- Payments are made.

- Tickets are picked up or mailed. (I would work to make this more exciting than just sending the tickets in the mail, or a cold pickup at the Will Call window. How about a special party? Or maybe create a special area for ticket pickup, decorate it, and give out some small items?)

Post-Buy Mini-Steps

- Schedule several meetings during the season to sit down and make sure the program is on track. (This can depend on whether you have a dedicated service team. However, I'd still contact the client myself for referrals.)

- Sending a special gift from the team or letter from a coach is always nice.

- Make sure the client is going through the ticket "maximization" program (something we covered in Chapter 6 in the interview of Paul Andrews of the Denver Nuggets).

Note: Remember to pick a "Start Date" when planning.

3. BUSINESS ACCOUNTING SERVICES

Tangible "To-Do" Tasks (just a few to give you some ideas)

- Agreement signed for services to be rendered

- Acquiring financial records from client

- Agree on deliverables and fiscal timelines

Special Events to Which to Invite Clients Early On

- Is there a free quarterly workshop you can hold or sponsor, either given by someone from your group on accounting and money management issues, or perhaps given by another professional from a related field (such as insurance or investments)? This could be something to which you invite past clients as well as new clients.

- Are there related seminars or workshops being held in your market to which you could invite prospective clients, or for which you could just buy the tickets and send them as your guests? If they accept your invitation, it's a sign they're serious, and reciprocity may kick in and make them feel obligated to move forward in the process.

Steps to Get the Client More Excited or Perhaps to Make Better Decisions

- Set up a financial strategy session with people from your office, and maybe invite some investment people you work with

- Schedule a meeting at the client's office to meet other key personnel, talk with employees, understand the product, etc. Too few accounting firms I've ever worked with take the time to find out the inner workings of my business or meet my colleagues. I think it's an important part of bonding.

Steps to Secure Inventory, Production, or Delivery Times

- Not sure accounting services could develop much here other than perhaps a more defined priority system for getting work done around tax time.

Steps to Help Fulfill the Order

- Get client's financial information into your systems

- Define the work to be done and time-lines

- Clearly communicate fee structure and payment requirements

- Sign any agreements or additional paperwork necessary for the work to get started

Post-Buy Mini-Steps:

- Send a special business-related gift to the client just after signing the deal. Business books are good for this purpose.

- Schedule quarterly check-in meetings, and put them on the calendar. (Don't just talk about them.)

- Now that you know something about the client and her business, send her occasional articles or books on her area of interest (business or personal).

Note: Remember to pick a "Start Date" when planning.

4. REAL ESTATE SALES

Tangible "To-Do" Tasks (just a few, to give you some ideas)

- Sign realtor agreement to represent client

- Get information into Multiple Listing Service

- Schedule open house events

Special Events to Which to Invite Clients Early On

- Sponsor regular free workshops entitled something like, "10 Factors to Think About When Considering Selling Your House." If you don't want to put this event on, find out about similar offerings in the area and then invite clients to attend with you, or send them as your guest.

Steps to Get the Client More Excited or Perhaps to Make Better Decisions

- Most good realtors do an initial exploratory meeting with clients to determine their needs, their hopes, and their wishes for the future, but I feel they should give the process a name, one that conveys the purpose of the meeting. For example, you could call it a "Home Listing Analysis Process" or a "Pre-Listing Profile." When you give things a name they become more special, and start to separate you from the competition.

Steps to Secure Inventory, Production, or Delivery Times

- Timing is always an issue with real estate, so good realtors take advantage of that and encourage clients to make decisions based on the timing of the market.

- Make a case for early commitment leading to more favorable open house weekends. Since a realtor can only be in one place at a time, say something like, "Even though I have multiple open houses going on every weekend, I like to highlight one where I spend a bit more time, and I like to put on a free barbecue, hand out special gifts, and so on. But I have to schedule that pretty far in advance, since I like to get every client into that rotation at least once."

- Use the busy schedule of a really good home appraiser to help commit the client to taking early action.

Steps to Help Fulfill the Order

- Paperwork is in
- Listing information is up
- Sign is in yard

Post-Buy Mini-Steps

- Send special gifts to the client upon signing the deal, perhaps something related to the lifestyle choice they're making (moving to a new area, or into a smaller or larger place).

- Schedule meetings on a regular basis. This is a major area of complaint when people are upset with their realtor. ("We never see him or hear from him.") I'd make sure that doesn't happen right from the start with some pre-scheduled meetings, even if you set them somewhat loosely on a weekly or monthly basis (depending on how long the average house stays on the market in your area). Say, for example, "You can plan on hearing from me at least during the last weekend of every month. I'll call or e-mail you and we can pick a time."

Note: Remember to pick a "Start Date" when planning.

5. COMPUTER / SOFTWARE SALES

Tangible "To-Do" Tasks (just a few, to give you some ideas)

- Plan installation dates
- Establish payment plan
- Set up training plan

Special Events to Which to Invite Clients Early On

- Develop a workshop for clients considering purchase of a certain computer or software? (Perhaps it's something that could be sponsored by the computer or software manufacturer?) These could be held on a regular basis so that salespeople can always invite prospective clients.

- Hold a complimentary orientation meeting for new buyers only. You could make it open for a certain number of participants from each client, and make it an exclusive offer, so pre-booking is a must.

Steps to Get the Client More Excited or Perhaps to Make Better Decisions

- Set a time to come in and do an impact study for their internal buying group. Perhaps this is simply a presentation you develop on the pros and cons of switching from their existing processes to your product, and some projections on what the world can look like three to five years from now.

- If it's applicable and would have a positive impact, invite clients to your office, especially if they can see production or talk with engineers. If you simply have office space, think about turning that space into a presentation center, where you could bring clients in and do a nice presentation or play an instructional video. An example from the sports industry is the "mock suite" that a team builds in their office because the actual stadium suites aren't completed yet, and they want to client to experience what they are like more than just through pictures and words on a page.

Steps to Secure Inventory, Production, or Delivery Times

- Place the order and set up the installation date. If you have tight installation and production timelines, you'll want to use that to get clients to book tentative dates.

- Set up training schedules. If clients want to get the best training times, or the best trainers, does it help to get their name in early? If so, then use that to your advantage and develop a priority list.

Steps to Help Fulfill the Order

- Install computers or software system

- Get final payment and/or payment plan

- Test system

- Set initial training date

Post-Buy Mini-Steps

- Is there a gift appropriate for the whole office? An office gift might be perfect for a computer or software sale since there is usually more than one person using the product. Food always works well for this, or something that will sit on everyone's desk, like a mouse pad or a coffee cup.

- Set up the post-installation training program.

- Schedule a post-buy review with the buyer group to make sure needs are met and everything is going along fine.

- Schedule regular meeting times during the year to review how the program and systems are working, and to make possible upgrades as they become available.

Note: Remember to pick a "Start Date" when planning.

6. MORTGAGES

Tangible "To-Do" Tasks (just a few to give you some ideas)

- Application

- Good faith estimate

- Financial information (taxes, etc.)

Special Events to Which to Invite Clients Early On

- Could you develop a free workshop for individuals who are thinking of refinancing in the next three to six months? These could be held at regular intervals every other month, or every quarter. The information provided could help homeowners make better decisions, avoid getting ripped off, etc. A similar workshop could be developed for new home buyers as well. These workshops can also be done online through phone or web conferencing.

- I'm not sure how feasible this is (remember these are just ideas to get you thinking), but what if you were to develop some sort of special event where you're touring new home projects, or perhaps home remodeling or home decorating projects, and turn it into some sort of fun party/social gathering: sort of like your own "Parade of Homes" (our local tour event of feature homes in the Denver area). Could you identify new home projects in your area, contact them and ask about using their area club house or the new model homes to host a gathering, then invite past clients and new prospects to meet, have some food and drinks, and get a special VIP tour of the home projects?

For home remodeling projects, or home decorating, are there good clients you have who wouldn't mind hosting a get-together to show off a new home addition, or major decorating project they've completed through refinancing or a second mortgage? They would have to be fairly substantial projects, but would definitely be unique if you could pull it off.

Steps to Get the Client More Excited or Perhaps to Make Better Decisions

- Develop easy-to-read tip sheets that help different buyer types (first time home buyers, re-fi's, second mortgage, etc.) make better decisions. Are there things they should do to avoid getting ripped off? Should they take additional steps to save money? Is there additional research they should be doing?

- You could develop a planning guide for the various client types, similar to the ones the post office gives out when you're considering a move. Full of helpful tips and steps, you should be thinking about 60-days out, 30-days out, 10-days out, etc. If the situation is right, you could designate someone in your office as "special advisor," someone who visits with the different client types to help with planning.

Steps to Secure Inventory, Production, or Delivery Times

- Get a "Good Faith Estimate" in place.

- Set up meetings with other internal people, or third-party services, the potential homeowner, or re-fi homeowner needs to interact with (e.g. appraiser, special advisor, accounting, etc.).

Steps to Help Fulfill the Order

- Application

- Information from appraisal

- Financial information

- Answers to special requests

Post-Buy Mini-Steps

- Set up a "post-closing" meeting to review the overall experience, make sure everything went smoothly.

- Pencil clients into your quarterly fun events, or special golf tournaments, or tours of homes, etc.

- Get their information so they'll continue and receive your company newsletter, or online offerings. Depending on regulations, are there other business introductions or recommendations you can make to help out your customer?

Note: Remember to pick a "Start Date" when planning.

7. PHARMACEUTICAL SALES

(Note: This sales process is probably one of the more unique ones, since there isn't much interaction that happens outside of the quick pop-in visits within the doctor's office.)

Tangible "To-Do" Tasks (just a few to give you some ideas)

- Determine schedule for seeing doctors.

- Understand the rep-visit protocol for each office.

Mini-Steps Pharmaceutical Reps Could Develop in Their
Unique Process

- The steps you develop should be toward forming
  the best relationship you can with a doctor in the
  thirty-second window you're given. Things I would
  put in a time-line would be:
  - Do I have a quick sketch of each doctor?
    - Where they're from, where they attended
      college and med school, family, hobbies,
      etc.? (Note: Be sensitive to the fact that
      some people don't want to go there.
      Don't force it. You can keep the relation-
      ship on the professional surface level ini-
      tially then move deeper later.)
  - Do I know what each doctor values in a rep?
    - What do they want to see? How often
      would they like to see me? What types
      of samples can I provide? What sorts of
      information are helpful (in what form –
      written, audio, etc.)? YOU MUST RE-
      CORD AND REMEMBER THIS IN-
      FORMATION (the most critical of all
      info in trying to form a relationship).
    - Have I sent the doctor professional infor-
      mation (books, reports, etc.) that will
      help further his understanding of a par-
      ticular condition?
    - Have I sent the doctor something to add
      value on a more personal note (assuming

again that you are trying to form this type of relationship) – an online link on fly fishing, an interesting article on raising teens in suburbia, etc. In an era when it's very tough to even invite doctors out for a social event, these types of more personal touches may be helpful.

- Do I have a relationship with others in the office?
  - Do I know names? Have I or do I share some personal information (if applicable)? Am I sensitive to their "rep visit procedures" when I walk in?

Mini-Steps in Closing

- This is one area where hard-sell, pushy closing strategies will probably backfire, mainly because you're going to have to go back in there on a regular basis (and getting access is already tough enough), and it's tough to talk a doctor into something she's not totally comfortable with recommending to a patient. At the same time, this is one sale where the seller isn't really sure they've "closed" on *anything* at the end of a visit, other than a verbal from the doctor: "Okay, if this condition comes up, I'll give it a try."

- I would recommend closing through hypothetical situations (something reps in other fields should also do) and then being particularly aware that doctors may be saying anything to just get rid of reps, or to avoid conflict.

SALESPERSON: "Dr. Arellano, you said you'll be seeing some of your anxiety and hypertension patients in the next several weeks . . . at this point, what would your comfort level be in using our product?"

DOCTOR: "Well, I'll certainly consider it if it's testing at the levels you're recommending."

SALESPERSON: "Okay, good. Just so I get a good understanding of the situation, can you give me a level of comfort at this point on a scale of 1 to 10, with 10 being most comfortable?

DOCTOR: "Yeah, I'd say I'm probably an 8, only because I haven't recommended it yet. But I like what I've heard from my colleagues here."

SALESPERSON: "All right. So sounds like there are several things you like about it. Are there things you're not completely comfortable with?"

DOCTOR: "Well, there is one thing. . . ."

The ability to share reality, even when it's ugly, is the basis for forming lasting relationships. I'd rather hear the issues that may exist, and try to deal with them than pretend they aren't there, and end up not making the sale.

The Impact of
Prospecting on Closing

This is not a book on prospecting, but we need to address the topic at least a bit because it does have a direct impact on consultative salespeople and our ability to close.

Let's just get at the heart of the issue: If we don't have enough irons in the fire, all the great closing strategies in the world will only help so much. If we aren't effectively prospecting and finding enough qualified prospects to load into the sales funnel each month, then it doesn't matter whether we close 100 percent of what we've got—if what we've got is only 50 percent of what we need.

I consult with salespeople and sales organizations all the time that do just enough prospecting to barely survive. They give themselves a margin of error that is so slight, they're living in a constant state of pressure and fear. For instance, they have to have twenty customers buy each month, and they go into the month with eighteen prospects, assuming that maybe two will come from somewhere. I equate it to climbing a 10-foot wall using a 9-foot ladder. Not only is it very shaky and dangerous standing on the top rung, but you've got to get lucky and have something fall from the sky in order for you to make your numbers and clear the wall.

I've always preached the concept of building a 20-foot ladder and increasing the margin of error with more prospects going in the funnel. I mean how much more fun would your life in sales be if you walked into the month with forty prospects, knowing you only had to close twenty to hit your number? This is particularly true if you're going to be more realistic and forthright with a YES or NO attitude on opportunities in your sales pipeline. You will need more prospects if you're going to bring more things to closure and not allow opportunities to sit and fester forever.

UNDERSTANDING PIPELINE REALITIES

The reality is that numbers don't lie, and new business development is a numbers game. And it doesn't matter whether you've got more of a relationship-based, referral-only type of process—where you don't do much cold calling at all—or whether most of your business comes from tons of cold-call prospecting: It's still a numbers game, with X amount of new opportunities going into the front of your pipeline, and X number of closes coming out.

There are many factors that must be applied when calculating our true pipeline performance:

- The number of closed pieces of business you need each month.

- Where your leads typically come from: cold calls, referrals, supplied leads, etc.

- The current length of your sales cycle (roughly how long it takes from going into the pipeline to successful exit, assuming you're going to shorten the cycle quite a bit by using the strategies in this book).

- The current closing percentages (assuming your skills will improve in this area as well).

Because this isn't a book on prospecting, I'm only going to cover some basic thoughts and strategies on developing some starting pipeline numbers. I strongly suggest you continue this process on your own.

Start at the End and Work Backwards

- Think about what it takes to get one new closed (for a YES) piece of business in the door.

- Go back and think about how many prospective clients had to be at the HOT level, in order to have one client go all the way to YES (normally the ratio is 3:1).

- Then move back one stage and think about how many WARM clients are needed to get one HOT prospect (normally the ratio is in the 3:1 to 4:1 range).

- Finally move back one more stage and think about how many COLD clients are needed to get one WARM prospect (normally the ratio is in the 5:1 to 6:1 range).

- So if your goal is to get five new clients, you'll just have to work the numbers backward:

> 5 New Clients
> 15 Hot Clients
> 45 Warm Clients
> 225 Cold Clients

• If this is what you need each month, it would translate into roughly ten new contacts per business day, along with the continued work on pushing Warm and Hot clients through the pipeline.

Again, your numbers will vary according to your own situation.

MEET THE "STEALTH KILLER": CALL RELUCTANCE

The problem at the core of poor prospecting and empty pipelines is Call Reluctance, or what I call the "Stealth Killer." Call Reluctance is tough to describe in short terms, but basically it's a mental condition that prevents us from picking up the phone or walking up to someone we've never met to introduce ourselves and our product or service, all out of fear: either fear of rejection, fear of the unknown, or a general fear that we should be doing something more productive with our time. It's a deadly disorder that anyone and everyone can catch, yet most people feel they're immune from it, and even deny it once it sets in and is destroying their career (thus the name "stealth killer").

When I do live workshops and seminars, I usually ask, "Who here suffers from occasional bouts of Call Reluctance?" Just a few hands will sheepishly be raised halfway in the air, until those honest folks look around and realize no one is doing it and they'll quickly drop their hands. Then I'll ask, "Okay, who NEVER gets Call Reluctance?" A few hands will boldly shoot in the air—almost always men, which I think is our lovely ego thing working. So then I'll ask, "Well, what about the rest of you? The 90 percent that didn't raise your hand to either question:

Either you get occasional bouts of Call Reluctance, or you never get it. Which is it?" Of course there are lots of blank stares, people looking around, some nervous chuckling, but no one really knows the right way to answer.

I think the reality is we're ALL susceptible to "catching" Call Reluctance, we're just not sure if it's an okay thing to admit to, especially in front of others. My feeling is that we need to face the beast head on and just admit we can catch the disease, thus opening the way to getting help.

"My name is Greg . . . and I have Call Reluctance." There . . . isn't that better?

Once you admit you can get it, and admit that you have it, you can get help from others around you, who perhaps will remind you that you've got a solid product to sell, or who may even sit with you while you call (two effective solutions I've discovered over the years).

There are a lot of great books and seminars on dealing with Call Reluctance, and I strongly encourage you to learn more about how to recognize it in yourself and in others, and then about what to do when it sets in.

For the purpose of this book, I'd like to move on with a simple acknowledgement that it's there, and that we need to deal with it. But now let's talk about some mistakes salespeople make in prospecting, and some immediate solutions that will help.

PROSPECTING MISTAKES

Prospecting Mistake 1: Salespeople Don't Have a Solid Strategy for Developing Enough Good Prospects

I find that, just as in closing, most salespeople don't have a solid strategy for finding enough good prospects. First of all, they haven't stopped long enough to think about who is a good prospect? Who belongs in the pipeline to begin with? Not everyone is "pipeline worthy." Just because someone can walk upright and fog a mirror doesn't mean they belong in our sales pipeline. We should have some baseline criteria for who is a good prospect. What are the base requirements of someone in your pipeline?

Part of our challenges with closing is that we've got too many prospects in the pipeline who have no business being there: They either aren't the right fit, don't have a need, aren't the right decision maker, aren't capable of paying, don't have an open mind to change, or generally aren't "closeable" within a certain time frame. If our pipelines are clogged with unqualified leads it certainly will have an impact on our closing ratio, mainly because we're going to spend even MORE time trying to turn a sow's ear into a silk purse—and that just can't happen.

Once we know who the good prospects are, is there a solid strategy for getting in front of enough of them? I find that generally salespeople work very hard and sincerely attempt to get enough "irons in the fire," but when I ask, "What is your strategy for getting enough good leads in the funnel?" they really aren't sure, it sort of just happens. And while many of them can survive on their gut instincts, I wonder how much more they could get accomplished—with even perhaps less effort—if they had a good strategy. Our prospecting strategy should answer these questions:

•   How am I going to target the "pipeline worthy" prospects?

      —Are there lists I can acquire?

      —Are there certain categories I can focus on?

•   How am I going to approach these prospects? What is the most effective pattern?

—For example, is the pattern: Call . . . call . . . e-mail information . . . call . . . call?

—Or is the pattern: E-mail . . . call. . . . e-mail information . . . call . . . e-mail?

• How can I network with more of these prospects?

• With what other noncompetitive product or service that already has these prospects as their clients could I perhaps form some sort of alliance?

Prospecting Mistake 2: Salespeople Don't Spend Enough Time Prospecting and They Don't Maximize Their Time

This is a big area, one that we can't fully address in this book, but one that should be discussed. Salespeople generally don't allocate enough time to developing new business, and in the time they DO spend, they're not fully maximizing their efforts.

Let's begin with scheduling. How much time you need to invest in business development is tied to your pipeline numbers and how many leads you need to add to the mix every week or month. Some people have the type of situation where they only need a few leads a month, while others need several new leads every day.

We need to take a step that only about 2 percent of the world's salespeople take (the top 2 percent, of course), and that is: putting your prospecting time in your calendar and treating it like you would any other appointment. If you leave prospecting to "whenever I can get some time," chances are (because of Call Reluctance) that you'll never "get some time" and end up blowing it off day after day, and week after week. Prospecting is, in a lot of ways, like working out: If you don't have a planned work-out schedule and stick to it on a regular basis, it won't be long till you're just somebody who used to work out:

• Determine how much time you need to invest each day, week, or month in prospecting.

• Block the time off on your calendar (the auto repeat function on electronic calendars is great for this).

• Get an accountability partner and maybe prospect together, or at least share with this person what you're going to do and get them to ask you about it from time to time.

As for maximizing the time you are spending, there are many strategies I could share with you, but within the context of this brief Appendix, here are just some quick tips:

• Create a separate "prospecting place," either in a separate room or in a separate area of your office or cubicle (even a different corner of the desk or in a certain desk drawer would work)—just a place where you keep all your prospecting "tools" (lists, notes, scripts, answers to objections, or prospect file). This helps with the change in mindset and focus required to pick up the phone and make calls. Even when you work for yourself, I'd suggest having a different place to go to prospect.

• Have goals in mind for each prospecting session, not just one big over all goal. If I'm running a marathon in six months, it's much easier to focus on what I need to accomplish today: let's say, focus on running 4 miles today versus focusing on the more than 26 miles I've got to run six months from now. It's easier to know whether your pace is on target if you focus on what you need to do each day in order to achieve the bigger goal.

• Try to make more "connected calls" versus "cold calls." The facts are that connected calls (defined as prospects with some sort of connection to a contact you currently have, or to a past contact, either through direct referral or some sort of loose reference point) are easier to make, more likely to end in a meeting, and much more likely to end up in a sale, than a freezing cold call.

Prospecting Mistake 3: Salespeople Stop Once They Experience a Little Success

This particular mistake is one of the hardest ones to understand IF you're unfamiliar with how the mind of a salesperson works to try and protect its owner. Just when the salesperson starts to see some success from her prospecting efforts—scheduling several new business meetings, creating proposals, etc.—she'll suddenly stop doing what she was doing to fill the pipeline. This mainly has to do with our strong, never-ceasing desire to avoid conflict and do the more comfortable and more productive tasks (or what we've told ourselves is more productive).

There is also a false sense of security that comes with what we perceive to be a full pipeline of prospects. It's like the farmer who thinks, "Well, I've got full silos now. Why do I have to plant again?" Of course, the reality is that the silos will be drawn down over time, and it takes time for seeds to become plants ready for harvest. The problem is we prefer the instant gratification that comes from watching crops grow and harvesting to the slow, painstaking exercise of planting little seeds in the cold, barren ground—not much instant gratification in planting.

Of course the irony in all of this is that we stop prospecting when we feel most confident, have lots of activity happening, feel great and powerful. Then, once our pipelines dry up, we get desperate and start prospecting when we're feeling panicky, nervous, anxious, and anything but confident. Our desire to avoid conflict only works temporarily, and we actually end up thrusting ourselves into an even greater conflict situation: prospecting when desperate.

Here are some quick tips for dealing with our "harvest-only mentality" and keeping our pipelines full:

• Make a minimum number of prospecting calls, even in the busiest of times, when you've got tons of proposals flowing and lots of client work to do. If you make even a couple of outreach calls a week, it will keep your prospecting muscles toned up (ever try working out after a three or four week layoff?) and keep a fresh trickle of new business prospects flowing into your pipeline on a regular basis.

• During busy times develop a list clients or prospects with whom you intend to make contact over a period of time (week or month) and take that list with you wherever you go. Keeping the names and numbers in front of you will make it easier to pick up the phone between meetings, or over lunch breaks, and will also be a great physical reminder of what you need to accomplish. Don't stop till you've checked all the names off the list.

• This is the perfect time—when you're feeling good about yourself and confident—to ask for more referrals and to work your network. This will keep a constant amount of new business opportunities floating to the surface and never let your pipeline go completely dry.

SOME THOUGHTS ON NETWORKING AND REFERRALS

Every person engaged in selling and business (especially consultative salespeople) should build a strong network, or as I like to call it, a NET that WORKS. For effective networking is a lot like fishing in the ocean: either you can stand alone on your boat casting one line into the massive sea, hoping for the right fish to come by, or you can cast a huge net over a large area, giving yourself fifty times the opportunity to catch the right fish, and many more to boot!

And what does all this have to do with Consultative Closing? Just about everything! For powerful networks will help identify many more qualified, willing prospects, who are easier and faster to close for a decision (especially a YES decision), who will usually commit to more, and who will turn into longer-lasting relationships that will create more additional sales and ongoing referrals.

In my years of working with salespeople and sales organizations to build better networks, I've noticed that most people think networking is simply getting out to the occasional business mixer, and staying in touch with people in your database. While that used to work back in the day, and still may work in some isolated instances or in really small communities, today's effective networkers are much more purposeful in their approach, and more effective in utilizing the latest technology. Here are some tips on effective networking:

• Purposely build the network with exactly whom you want. There is a difference between a network that you are purposely building to generate qualified leads, and one that is just a compilation of everyone you've ever met. Of course, there is nothing wrong with having thousands of contacts and friends in a huge database, and with reaching out to them on a regular basis. When you describe for your clients, friends, or other contacts in your network, who you're looking for as a good lead, make sure you talk about the symptoms, not the treatments. For example, if a doctor tells me he to look for people who could use Xygenomer-ixon, it means a lot less to me than if he said to look for people who can't sleep and imagine themselves as farm animals. I can recognize symptoms, I may not understand the treatments, or what the medicine is designed to do.

• While the networking groups and clubs are fine (like the chamber of commerce, or tips groups), I'm talking here about hand-selecting five, ten or even fifteen people, whom you want to form a leads-generating network. Pick people who have a great reputation and who call on the same types of prospects you do (but who obviously sell something different). With this group you will:

Communicate regularly

Share qualified leads back and forth

Make personal introductions, not just do massive lead-swaps

• Think about ways you can support your network, between the times they provide you with leads. There are several online resources that offer free information (articles, white papers, etc.) that you can quickly attach and send to everyone. And don't skimp on what you give your best lead providers for turning over great leads. Wouldn't they be more motivated to keep their eyes and ears open for you if they received a dinner for two at a nice restaurant or club seats at an NBA game as opposed to a token "finders fee" you may toss their way?

HOW TO ASK FOR REFERRALS

Referrals and personal introductions are critical to the success of consultative salespeople. Our relationships tend to be stronger, and we must take advantage of them to get more referrals if we're to survive and thrive.

Referrals and leads coming from a personal introduction are much more likely to buy, will buy more, and all with less work. They're also more trusting and more likely to form long-term relationships than are leads coming from a cold call.

Here are some tips for asking for referrals:

• Make sure it's not just a one-way street where you're always doing the asking. You should ask first what type of business your customer may be looking for, for this will pave the way for them to help you:

> "Maddy, I do a lot of networking. Tell me what type of clients you're looking for."

• Instead of asking questions that are too big, or too general, try to narrow the client's focus:

> *Too Big a Question:* "Do know anyone who could use my services?"

> *A Focused Question:* "Are there contacts within your organization who are also struggling with implementation issues?"

I strongly suggest that you look at your prospecting and business-development processes to make sure they're creating enough potential new business opportunities for you to succeed comfortably.

PROSPECTING SCRIPT TEMPLATE

This is the outline of a prospecting script I've used in several different industries. It features what I like to call the "confusion method," which is basically calling. Instead of pretending to know what is going on (which I normally don't), I'm calling and sharing the fact that I'm confused about what has happened in the past, and that we need to meet to clear up my confusion. This strategy works incredibly well because most people won't attack or kill a confused person.

Open (once past receptionist or screener)

> "Hi, _____(client name)_____, this is _____(your name)_____ with _____(your company name)_____."

Reason for the Call

> *"The reason for the call is to schedule a quick meeting with you over the next week to ten days. I just took over this area, and in looking through the little bit of information I have, it appears we've never done a Needs Analysis with your organization. Have you seen anyone from our company?"*

What Is a Needs Analysis?

> *"A Needs Analysis is a short meeting we do, where I'll ask a few questions about your organization, tell you a little about what we do, and see if there is any fit, and if we might be able to help you."*

Remove Pain or Provide Pleasure

- *Cut down on X.*
- *Stop losing on Y.*

- *Increase your Z.*
- *Bring More XX in the door.*

Are You Open?

"Are you open to new ideas in those areas?"

We Need to Meet (I use this phrase often in prospecting)

"Great! Then we need to meet. How does this Tuesday sound?"

Greg's Random Quick Tips for Salespeople and Sales Managers

On Buying Sales Training

- Understand that most one-time workshops are like cotton candy: Tastes great, fun to eat, but disappears in a flash, and soon the sugar buzz in gone. Long-term, consistent training is the key to long-term, consistent results.

- Management must attend and participate, or it will feel like punishment to the salespeople.

- Clarify expectations with the trainer, and ask the trainer to put some "skin in the game" with a percentage of his compensation tied to results (man, do my fellow trainers hate when I mention this one).

- Look for professional trainers and coaches, not just some guy who bought a training franchise. Nothing wrong with franchised programs, but make sure the person who is doing the training (whether using franchised material or not) is an effective trainer, coach, speaker, etc.

- As for sales training programs and systems I'd recommend, there are several sources for good information, and I think if you have an open mind, you can pick up something from any workshop or book. In addition to the "old standards" of Dale Carnegie, Tom Hopkins, and Zig Ziglar, I like the Sandler Sales System, as well as the concept SPIN Selling from Neil Rackham.

On Sales Automation Software

- Everyone should be using some sort of CRM (customer relationship management) tool. Trying to keep tons of client information in your head or on a spreadsheet is very challenging, and will lead to things dropping through the cracks.

- A CRM tool should have the following capabilities (in addition to the basics of storing client data and managing your calendar):
  —Should be able to record steps and stages in the sales process (our Mini-Steps), and then even attach a customizable percentage close to the attainment of those steps.
  —Should be able to track "work flow" and best practices, giving managers and sellers a clear and accurate look at where opportunities truly are in the sales pipeline.
  —Should have a robust forecasting capability.

- I've used several systems myself, but personally, I'm liking the Salesnet (a division of RightNow Technologies, Inc.®) product more and more.

On Resources and Information (just a few of the many out there)

- JustSell.com is a great source of free articles, ideas, and concepts.

- InfoUSA.com is the source I use for targeted prospect lists.

- Monster.com and SalesJobs.com are great for finding good folks.

- Raindance.com and Webex.com are both great for online conferencing.

- TVWorldwide.com for live streaming and developing video training.

Index

About the Author

Greg Bennett has been a top sales trainer, consultant, strategist, and coach since 1988. He has worked with hundreds of organizations and thousands of salespeople in a wide variety of industries, including extensive sales consultation  and strategy development for over 150 professional sports teams and major universities across the United States and Canada.

His strategies and techniques are considered by many to be the most realistic, user-friendly and "street smart" available anywhere. He focuses on the fundamentals of sales success, with a special emphasis on what he calls "Consultative Closing" strategies—designed to help consultative sellers, business owners, and professionals become more effective closers.

In 1998, Bennett developed the first online sales training site, www.SalesTrainingTV.com, and began using the Internet to revolutionize the way training programs could be delivered to sales managers and salespeople on the front lines.

Bennett is also partner in a sports-consulting and branded-product-development company called APC (Altitude Profit Consulting), a partner organization within Kroenke Sports Enterprises, owners of the Denver Nuggets, Colorado Avalanche, Colorado Rapids, and several other sports and entertainment entities. APC also develops sales-related promotional products and apparel for pro teams and corporations.

He lives in Colorado with his wife, Rosemary, and four daughters, Brooke, Blaire, Kaity, and Madison.

Bennett offers several live and online training and support programs for large, medium, and small sales organizations and small businesses. For more information, please contact:

APC
(Altitude Profit Consulting)
917 Auraria Parkway
Denver CO 80204
Toll Free: 866-405-5525
E-mail: info@APCProfit.com
www.APCProfit.com